gracious space

Working Better Together

by **Patricia M. Hughes**

with **Bill Grace**

Second Edition

Center for
Ethical Leadership
www.ethicalleadership.org

Gracious Space: Working Better Together
Written by Patricia M. Hughes with Bill Grace
Series Editor: Jeremy Stringer

Graphic Design: Gylan Green
Center for Ethical Leadership Founder: Bill Grace
Executive Director: Dale Nienow

Published by The Center for Ethical Leadership
1401 E. Jefferson St., Suite 505
Seattle, WA 98122
www.ethicalleadership.org

First Printing, May 2004
Second Printing, October 2007
Third Printing, September 2008
Second Edition, June 2010
Second Printing, June 2011

Printed in the United States of America
ISBN 978-0-9755440-1-3

Book pages printed with soybean ink on 40% post-consumer recycled content.

table of contents

Foreword and Introductions 4

Part One: What Is Gracious Space 14

    A Spirit of Compassion and Curiosity 17

    A Setting That Is Expressed Externally 24

    A Commitment To Invite the Stranger 28

    A Commitment To Learn In Public 37

    A Container for Working With Conflict 43

    A Tool To Promote the Common Good 48

Part Two: Creating Gracious Space 65

    Building Trust 65

    Inquiry and Deep Listening 73

    Challenges of Gracious Space 82

Part Three: Gracious Space in Action 85

    Personal Applications 85

    Organizational Applications 87

    Community Applications 89

Appendix 95

foreword

A friend and colleague recently commented that for a year she focused her meditation and journal writing on "becoming a more gracious person." My attention was arrested by her choice of the word "gracious." Why did she aspire to become more gracious, when she might have chosen to become more loving or compassionate, thoughtful, kind, ethical, spiritual, or wise? There is a long list of worthy virtues, strengths, and capacities that might serve as the focus of a year's disciplined intent.

I began to recognize, however, that the word "gracious" stands in courageous contrast to what some call the "coarsening" of our society. We live in a time when many suffer the accelerated pace of life we call busyness—a condition that demands "efficiencies" and justifies the erosion of relationships that most sustain and nourish our lives in the homeplace and the workplace. Simultaneously, we undergo an incessant escalation of violence in political and entertainment media along with the hardening of competitive, polarizing forces that relentlessly conspire to determine who is included and who is excluded. In this context, the word "gracious," as my friend was choosing to embody it, was clearly a bid for a different mode of being—a willingness "to make more gentle this cruel world."

As the dictionary reveals, "gracious" can mean merely a superficially charming or tasteful appearance, a facile, affable, genial desire to please and even impress. I knew, however, that my friend was claiming the word "gracious" as a pathway to a deeper, more challenging, and more profound place. "Gracious" can also signify kindness, mercy, tact, compassion, a desire to understand—a generosity of spirit. The practice of graciousness is an invitation to qualities of being that move us into more meaningful, productive, nourishing, and just relationships.

The Center for Ethical Leadership is dedicated to fostering relationships that allow the human community to truly flourish. They have taken the word "gracious" beyond its usual association with an individual person or a particular act and have developed a practice of "creating gracious space" in which even organizations and communities may become "gracious."

Creating gracious space as they practice it, means attending to the physical space in terms of its comfort and aesthetic. But more, gracious space becomes a way of speaking of what Winnicott, Kegan, and Heifetz among others have described as a "holding environment" that makes it possible for people to trust enough, be vulnerable enough, be conflictual enough, and to be curious enough—curious together about what is yet possible, what can be healed, learned, and created that has not yet been imagined.

It is particularly notable that in the practice of gracious space the Center has learned a key element is the presence of "the stranger." The importance of hospitality to the stranger is rooted in an ancient wisdom that spans many cultures. In today's world, we know that justice is a matter of who is included and excluded in the dialogue. We are learning that if we are going to find more adequate manifestations of the common good, then positive, constructive encounters with "otherness"—those outside our own tribe—are essential. When our encounters with "the stranger" (or simply the person or group we don't like so much) are truly gracious, an empathic bond across difference is formed. Seeing what the other sees, feeling something of what the other feels, gives rise to compassion. Compassion gives rise to a conviction of possibility—"there has to be a way." And that conviction gives rise to the courage to risk, to create a more adequate justice and more prosperous and sustainable ways of life.

Surely we now stand at one of those times in history when the practice of gracious space is crucial. As we grapple with unprecedented conditions and tensions of dramatic import, the call to graciousness is a call to both soul and society. This monograph describes the creation of gracious space as a leadership tool, a technique, and also as a desire or way of being. If it is to become a way of being, we have work to do that begins in contemplation. This monograph can be an occasion for contemplation — the kind of deep listening both within and without that helps us see in new ways and takes us to places we didn't plan to go. The questions posed throughout this work can foster precisely that. Patricia Hughes and Bill Grace have created within this writing a very gracious space — an invitation to step into a greater participation in the cultivation of more compassionate, just, and peaceful ways of life.

Sharon Daloz Parks
Whidbey Island, WA
March 2004

words of thanks

Jim Emrich, director of the Servant Leader Association, first used the term "Gracious Space" with Center founder Bill Grace in 1996. The term captured Bill's imagination and he borrowed it for subsequent Center trainings. Gracious Space quickly became a significant concept in Center programs aimed at helping individuals develop leadership capacity and promote the common good.

Early renditions of the Gracious Space curriculum, tested with leaders from government agencies, neighborhood groups, corporations and in educational settings, were well received. We then introduced Gracious Space to groups struggling with conflict as a tool to find shared understanding and create solutions. Gracious Space is now helping many organizations and communities across the country to work better together.

Several individuals helped make this publication possible. Many participants in Center programs told us how they applied the tools and concepts personally and professionally.

Colleagues at the Center for Ethical Leadership were involved at many levels. Dale Nienow, Evelyn Correa and Judy Hansen helped test and refine the message of Gracious Space for organizations. Karma Ruder, Steve Stapleton, and Gylan Green consistently demonstrated Gracious Space in the workplace, and Bill Grace and Kathleen Hosfeld were attentive and supportive readers of the manuscript.

Thanks also go to Jennifer Madeoy, Mito Alfieri and Michelle Quigley Pearson, students in Barbara Sjoholm's 2003 Developmental Editing course in the University of Washington's Certificate Program in Editing for providing valuable attention and suggestions. Sharon Daloz Parks graciously agreed to write a foreword in the midst of her own busy writing schedule.

Lastly, the Center has great gratitude for Jeremy Stringer, the series editor for the Center's publications. Jeremy donated many hours editing this piece, and his vision helped craft it into a useful and inspiring work.

series editor
comments

As our world has become increasingly diverse, a key issue in organizations in both the business and nonprofit realms is how to unite people around common goals, in order to advance their shared agendas. Almost all groups find it necessary to reach hard to find ways of unifying people so they can effectively work together. Beyond the obvious racial, gender, and generational divides, coming to grips with intellectual diversity, or different ways of thinking, is a challenge for many individuals and groups.

Diversity "training" is a familiar component of staff development programs in many organizations. Gurus breeze in, offer some whiz-bang solutions, and depart. It may be stimulating, even inspirational, but - usually - the lessons fizzle in a fortnight.

Lasting organizational change, particularly in diverse groups, has to be internalized by participants. This type of change is not accomplished by short, though well-intended, training, or quick fixes designed for interchangeable audiences. Significant personal change must be accomplished before (or certainly along with) organizational change. Lasting improvement has to be able to be sustained after the trainers have flown home.

Into the search for a sustainable model of organizational improvement come Pat Hughes, Bill Grace and the Center for Ethical Leadership. The Center is concerned with bringing people together, giving voice to the previously unincluded, resolving conflicts within and among groups, and making decisions to benefit the "common good," not just for individual organizations, but also for our larger society. The Center strives to unite diverse groups to solve the problems they are facing in a non-adversarial manner, through specific learned behaviors and models.

The principles in this monograph provide a blueprint for bringing people together. They are based on the authentic truth that people must often start with themselves in order to bring about change in others. Pat and Bill have not written an infallible cookbook for establishing Gracious Space. Rather, they have given us a general map that can be adapted to individual circumstances. As readers begin to apply the principles in this monograph they can develop their own capacities for building Gracious Space into a powerful tool for both self-improvement and organizational change. Realistically, the authors allow the reader to start from his or her own place, and do not assume that all people have the same starting place in common.

This monograph has been written only after exhaustive "field testing" of the concepts that make up Gracious Space. Specific ideas have been honed by hundreds of people who attended the Center for Ethical Leadership's various workshops. Whether the reader has attended one of the center's programs and wants to begin to apply its concepts, or whether the reader is coming to the topics in the monograph for the first time, the authors provide both the conceptual underpinning and the practical application to guide the implementation of Gracious Space.

Perhaps the best test of the ideas in this monograph is whether or not they really work. I can attest that they do. An organization I was working with was filled with distrust and hostile communications. People refused to work together. In meetings some participants would sit on the other side of the room from their perceived adversaries, as far away as possible. Some would roll their eyes when others spoke, refuse to listen to differing opinions, and find every excuse imaginable to avoid resolving the underlying conflicts that were pulling the group apart. I was at my wit's end!

One of the leaders of the Center for Ethical Leadership told me about the concepts of Gracious Space. He offered to bring them into my group to try to heal our wounds and develop a greater sense of trust. The approach sounded to me to be authentically aimed at organizational improvement, in a way that would not stigmatize participants who in the past had refused to work together, but allow them to make progress toward developing a healthier community individually and collectively.

I had nothing to lose, so I brought the Center in for a seminar around Gracious Space. The transformation in my group was dramatic! As people warmed to the idea that they could play a role in creating the type of space (and organization) they dreamed of, differences among people gradually faded into the background and positive communications began to replace the negatively charged environment that was the norm before. When the seminar was over, we still had work to do, but the concepts we learned, and which are all here in this wonderful monograph, gave us new tools to use to continue to work toward developing the type of organization we wanted to have.

The ideas in this monograph may be applied to a group, like the one I was a part of, but they can also improve the quality of organizational life for individuals. As we open ourselves to really listen to others we establish stronger interpersonal bonds. And we inevitably build stronger, more positive and lasting communities. I encourage you to actively engage with this monograph, answering the questions in the journal as you go along, and practicing the principles explained. By taking the time to personalize the concepts in this monograph, you will get the most out of it. And you will be on your way to creating a healthier and more positive environment for yourself and others in both your personal and professional life.

Happy reading!
Jeremy Stringer
Seattle, WA
March, 2004

welcome

Oh the joy —
The inexpressible comfort
Of feeling safe with a person
Having neither to measure words
Nor weigh thoughts
Pouring them all out just as they are,
Chaff and grain together
Certain that a loving hand will sift through,
Keep what is worth keeping,
And with a breath of kindness —
Blow the rest away

> *— Dinah M. Craik*
> *Adapted from an Arabian proverb*

On the Flathead Indian Reservation in Montana, community leaders are trying to solve the problem of high school dropouts and a sense of hopelessness among their young people. In Seattle, Washington, employees at Seattle Public Utilities are striving to become a "world class" utility, providing citizens and the environment with reliable service and leadership. In St. Louis, Missouri, Boeing executives gather to learn the latest leadership tools for navigating in a complex, global business environment.

What do these people have in common? In each case, they are confronting complicated issues where the answers are not straightforward. They are considering diverse perspectives, multiple alternatives and new possibilities. They are on tight deadlines and budgets, and often have to make decisions without the benefit of complete information.

Whether the challenge is negotiating conflicts, creating new possibilities or planning for the future, we need an environment that is conducive to learning and working well together. We know intuitively that many minds are better than one when creating ideas and products, but too often we don't feel we have the luxury to take the time to involve others.

Gracious Space is an environment in which creative thinking and learning can occur. It inspires an attitude of openness, curiosity and discovery. It is a safe place, but one that also invites diverse opinion and can hold conflict. It sounds simple, but often it is hard to do.

What do we mean by Gracious Space?

The Center for Ethical Leadership believes that individuals, organizations and communities grow healthy in the environment provided by Gracious Space. We define Gracious Space as "a spirit and a setting where we invite the 'stranger' and embrace 'learning in public.'"

Gracious Space is a remarkably adaptive, foundational concept that can add value to many situations, whether in business, community groups or at home. It is a technique, but more, it is a way of being that shapes our interactions with others. Gracious Space is a highly effective leadership tool, but it is not limited to leadership or business settings. It is a framework for working with conflict, but it is not limited to conflict resolution. Rather, Gracious Space is a way to guide conflict towards transformation. It can be used to make a path for peace and new collaborations in any setting.

Gracious Space has the potential to transform the human heart. When we choose graciousness, we choose an approach that fosters understanding. We choose to be open-minded and welcoming of diverse opinions. This attitude grows within us and can be nurtured through practice.

The effects of Gracious Space can be profound when we allow it to move beyond an intellectual approach or leadership skill. The poem above conveys the kindness and openness that speak directly to the power of Gracious Space. This ethic of care sets Gracious Space apart from other group process or conflict resolution approaches.

Gracious Space is also an important part of a journey to advance the common good. In the presence of Gracious Space, individuals improve the quality of their relationships, groups learn to value the different talents and perspectives of their members, and whole organizations and communities become continuous learners, applying mutual respect and creativity to some of their most intractable problems.

Personally, Gracious Space has come to embody a spirit, a set of skills and an approach to leadership and life that I truly believe in.

I have used it successfully at home, at work and in the community. Gracious Space can produce unexpected and profound results in our relationships with others, and infuse our work with new meaning. I enthusiastically share these ideas with emerging and existing leaders.

Who needs Gracious Space?

The purpose of this publication is to teach individuals and groups to use Gracious Space to the best advantage. It is written for those who want to bring more openness and creativity to their work. It is for leaders who must make decisions without all the information. It is for groups struggling with conflict, difficult issues and divergent viewpoints. It is for people who don't think of themselves as leaders, but who are role models – parents, coaches and employees – and shape the world around them through their actions. This latter group – the Center calls them small "l" leaders – can use Gracious Space at home, at work and in the community to connect with relatives or explore issues with colleagues, friends and neighbors.

We all could use some Gracious Space. Today's world is fast and complex. Problems are often connected to each other in puzzling ways that require a systemic response. Ideas and people move quickly. Just 20 years ago we enjoyed long lunch hours and time to chat with neighbors from the front porch. In these fast-forwarded times, relationships can suffer and opportunities for creative dialogue are often snuffed by deadlines and overbooked schedules. We all need a time and place to slow down and listen to ourselves and others.

We need Gracious Space because leaders at all levels today have more data available to them than ever before. They need to be skilled at synthesizing vast amounts of information and sorting conflicting opinions before choosing the best path. This approach takes time and energy. It requires restraint to think *before* acting. But when the solution is ambiguous and the problems are complex, we need more resources to determine the best course of action. More than ever before, today's leaders must be learners. They need to bring open minds to complex situations and create environments where different ideas and alternatives can be explored and understood. Gracious Space is that environment. In it we can question, collaborate, learn, and act with greater clarity and confidence.

How should I use this book?

- **Part One.** This section describes the meaning of Gracious Space, and when it is most needed and useful. It includes a description of the spirit of Gracious Space, how to create a setting that evokes Gracious Space, the concept of inviting the "stranger," and the practice of learning in public.

- **Part Two.** This section explores tools for building trust, models for inquiry and deep listening, and possible challenges to creating Gracious Space. Tools reviewed include the Johari Window, Dialogue, Skillful Discussion and Appreciative Inquiry.

- **Part Three.** This section documents recent situations where Gracious Space has been used successfully by individuals, organizations and community groups.

- **Appendix.** This section provides additional references that support the reader and leader in creating Gracious Space. Resources include a Gracious Space Self-Assessment and a Guide for Getting Started.

Throughout the publication we have provided a *Gracious Space Journal.* These are a series of reflective questions to help generate ideas and actions that can bring Gracious Space to life.

part one:

what is gracious space?

"Leadership isn't hitting people over the head.
That's assault, not leadership."

— *Dwight D. Eisenhower*

At seminars on Gracious Space, we often ask participants to think about what the term means to them. Have they ever been in a space that feels gracious? Can they identify characteristics that make Gracious Space unique? Previous participants responded in this way:

- "It's a place where I can give my opinions without criticism"

- "People have deep respect for differences here"

- "It's where you hold off on judgment for a while"

- "It's stepping back and reflecting on my assumptions"

- "I'm curious and willing to be influenced"

- "It's all about slowing down and really listening"

Several people have fondly recalled the warmth of the family kitchen. One person said, "Gracious Space is like grandma's house – you get milk and cookies but no lectures." The people we work with realize there is something special about Gracious Space. They immediately grasp the difference between Gracious Space and the rushed, often adversarial exchanges that make up much of their days.

Many people feel trapped in polite but superficial discussions, or they feel shut down and are afraid to share their ideas. Hundreds of Center seminar participants have said they want less defensive conversations with family and neighbors; they want trusting, open relationships that help them learn; they want to work in environments that bring forth their best ideas and fully use their talents. Consider the following examples:

- Rose has attended her family's annual reunion for ten years. Recently she has started to dread them because her aunt asks personal questions, like why isn't she married and when is she moving back "home." Rose loves her family, but feels her aunt is not treating her with respect. She might skip the reunion this year.

- Rebra supervises a busy customer service center and has had difficulty getting support from her staff. During a recent evaluation, she learned her staff views her as aloof and unavailable. Rebra admits she is shy and task-focused, but didn't realize these traits were perceived negatively. She wants to improve her relationship with her staff and work better as a team.

- A school district wants to provide better education in a racially diverse community. There are many different expectations and opinions to consider, and the school leaders fear their effort to unite the segregated members of the community could disintegrate into a shouting match.

These examples demonstrate the thorny situations we often find ourselves in. They show how good people in difficult situations can be tempted to revert to communication patterns that fracture and disconnect, when what they really want is to bring together. The examples indicate a need for a different way of being together. At seminars on Gracious Space, participants often sigh at the characteristics that describe Gracious Space, and say, "Wouldn't that be nice?"

Gracious Space can help. It fosters a spirit of learning and gives people a new way to communicate. It cultivates an open space and time where people are unafraid, and where the emphasis is on the exchange of ideas, not on being right. There is increased trust among the people involved and a willingness to share information. In Gracious Space, creative, effective outcomes emerge that are not possible in a more hasty or combative environment.

Gracious Space has two dimensions: a "spirit," or an inner life that one nurtures within oneself; and a "setting," or an outer expression with others. Gracious Space has two commitments: inviting the stranger, and learning in public. In this first section we explore these dimensions and commitments of Gracious Space.

gracious space journal

What is Gracious Space?

1. *Have I ever been in a situation that felt like Gracious Space? What was the situation? What was happening that made it feel gracious?*

2. *What are some of the adjectives that describe Gracious Space? What does Gracious Space mean to me?*

3. *What are some definitions of Gracious Space from the members of my group or family?*

4. *How can these definitions create a culture of Gracious Space for our group, workplace or community?*

5. *What situations am I involved in that could benefit from Gracious Space?*

a spirit of compassion and curiosity

"Be the change you want in the world."

— *Mahatma Gandhi*

When people begin to work with Gracious Space, they soon recognize that a spirit of Gracious Space needs to reside within before they can create it externally and invite others into it. The inner life of Gracious Space is a spirit an individual develops and carries within him or herself. It means having trust and a desire to learn, being open, vulnerable, curious, and compassionate. These personal traits are seeds that enable Gracious Space to blossom inside. We all have them; some emerge spontaneously while others need to be nurtured.

The Buddhist teacher Thich Nhat Hanh, nominated by Martin Luther King Jr. for the Nobel Prize, says we must "be the peace" we wish to see in the world. Hanh, as well as Gandhi and King before him, believes change begins within.

The first step to having a "spirit" of Gracious Space is to become aware of our natural tendencies toward Gracious Space and how we perceive the world. Is each day a battle or something to embrace with joy? Do we have patience and curiosity about things we don't understand? Do we feel rushed? What happens when we try to slow down? Do we have compassion for others and for ourselves? How do we show compassion? How do we react during a bad day or week or year?

These questions can help identify some innate strengths of Gracious Space as well as what might be areas we want to improve. Refer to the Self Assessment in the Appendix to clarify additional characteristics of Gracious Space. For most people, it takes commitment and practice to nurture an inner spirit of Gracious Space, but anyone can create new habits and increase their sense of graciousness with a little intention.

For example, one woman discovered that an inner source of graciousness could improve her relationship with a colleague.

"Liz" worked with a person who was highly intuitive, but very opinionated and prone to making quick, negative judgments. Liz found it difficult to work with this person and invented ways to work around him so she would not be subjected to his constant criticisms. But she knew this was irresponsible and unproductive in the long run, so she decided to try an experiment. During their next conversation she would approach him from a place of unconditional acceptance and compassion. She would open her heart and mind, listen deeply, be patient, and try to understand his point of view. The next day, she tried it.

Five minutes into the meeting, her colleague abruptly stopped talking and looked at her.

"What are you doing?" he asked.

"I'm...just...listening," Liz said.

A silent moment passed. Liz felt something important had happened, as if he sensed her inner calm. She felt the tension dissolve, and then they continued talking. Liz was stunned at his response to her experiment.

"I didn't do anything other than deeply listen, with a heart of compassion, regardless of his faults and whether I agreed with him," Liz said. "He picked up on that and it changed things between us."

From that point forward her colleague trusted Liz more, sought her opinions and even began to imitate her patient, curious approach to conversations. They collaborated more and made better decisions for the organization. Needless to say, work was much more enjoyable and satisfying for Liz.

Liz's story shows that being compassionate can significantly impact a relationship, *even if the other person is unaware of your intentions or is uncooperative.* Her experience also demonstrates how being curious creates openness and influence in situations where one might not necessarily have power or control. Liz nurtured a spirit of compassion and curiosity, and this spirit changed her relationship and work environment.

Intention feeds a spirit of Gracious Space

Sometimes the capacity to "be" Gracious Space is instinctive. More often it is deliberate, and needs to be mastered over time through practice and patience. David Sando, an engineering manager at Boeing

in Kent, Washington discovered how the importance of being intentional in his interactions with others. "I began to hold the concept of
Gracious Space in my mind whenever I encountered a difficult interpersonal or group situation," he said. "Constant practice has been the key
for me because emotions can quickly derail Gracious Space, especially
if you feel like you are being attacked."

Many people ask how they can preserve Gracious Space in the
face of someone who is unyielding, unwilling to return the graciousness, or just grouchy. Most of us know and work with people like this,
and sometimes entire institutions can adopt an uncooperative person-
ality.

Fred Kofman, founder of Leading Learning Communities and an
organizational consultant and teacher, makes the point that we can
choose how we behave regardless of others' choices. He says it is our
decision how we want to be in the world, as opposed to taking an "I
will if you will" approach.

"Consciousness is the capacity to observe, choose, and act in
accordance with your values," he states. "And 'conscious business'
means using that ability at every level of your work: in being aware
of the needs of others and expressing your own; in seeing the hidden
emotional obstacles that may be holding your team back; in making
good decisions under pressure; and even delving into "spiritual" questions such as 'Who am I?' and 'What is my real purpose here?'"

There is no magic wand to instill graciousness in ourselves, and
it is impossible to force someone to give us Gracious Space. If we want
more Gracious Space, we have to develop it within ourselves. The key
to doing this is to tap a source that is constant, personal and immune
to the ups and downs of others' moods and actions.

While Gracious Space is not intended to be a religious term, it
often evokes a spiritual awareness in people. Developing an inner life
of Gracious Space complements the teachings of many spiritual tra-
ditions, and "grace" is a significant concept in most major religions.
Many people have discovered their source of graciousness in the habit
of daily meditation or prayer.

Jah'Shams Abdul-Mumim runs the Non-Traditional Leadership Institute for adolescent boys and young men in Los Angeles. His goal is
to funnel the energy and leadership potential of these youth away from
gangs into more positive outlets. His inner commitment to Gracious
Space helped him connect his faith to his leadership.

"Because I am increasingly thrust into leadership roles I take every opportunity to find solitude, be still, and begin the process of deep personal reflection," Jah'Shams said. "Through this reflection I developed a personal mission statement that involves deep inner growth and becoming a spiritually conscious leader. I have recommitted myself to a powerful process of transformation that enables me to experience new possibilities and completely engage in the service of God and humanity. To me, this is Gracious Space."

Compassion nourishes a spirit of Gracious Space

The roots of the word compassion can help us dig a little deeper into the spirit of Gracious Space. The word compassion stems from the Latin *com*, meaning "together" and *pati,* meaning "suffer." When we have compassion, we "suffer with" another. Compassion is extending our concern to other beings, especially those who are most vulnerable and least fortunate.

At the Center for Ethical Leadership, we believe that individuals can learn compassion by being of service to others. When we serve those who are hungry, poor, or who have troubles far greater than our own, we become students of their suffering. As we serve, we learn. We feel the sufferings and desires of others and feel an urge to help.

Joanna Macy, a scholar of Buddhism and general systems theory, tells about a lesson in compassion while traveling in the Himalayan foothills. One day, she noticed a fly in her tea. She wasn't particularly worried, having lived abroad among various insects for years. But her companion, a young monk-in-training, took her cup outside and extracted the fly.

"When he reentered the cottage he was beaming," Macy wrote. 'He is going to be all right,' he told me quietly. He explained how he had placed the fly on a leaf of a bush where his wings could dry. I could not, truth to tell, share his dimensions of compassion, but the pleasure in his face revealed how much I was missing by not extending my self-concern to *all* beings, even flies. Yet the very notion that it was possible gave me boundless delight."

Compassion is an important element of Gracious Space because it enables us to get into another's shoes, if only for a moment, and to understand their perspective. Compassion is what moves Gracious Space beyond mere technique. When we feel compassion, we truly care about the other person's situation. With compassion, our conversations are softer, our relationships more meaningful and our work together more fruitful.

People who tap their inner source and internalize Gracious Space will carry it wherever they go. It comes with them when they enter a room and shapes the questions they ask and the approaches they take. They will be more compassionate and intentional in all situations, even those that lack grace, and they will not easily be pushed off their center. We must *be* that which we want to create.

Curiosity enables a spirit of Gracious Space

Being intentional, compassionate and guided by a spiritual practice help us nurture an inner spirit of Gracious Space. Being curious is another element that feeds the spirit of Gracious Space. When we speak of curiosity, we do not mean voyeurism; nor do we mean an idle, passing level of interest. We do not mean the passive curiosity that frequently occurs in the workplace, when someone offers a differing viewpoint and others sit back to watch what happens.

The curiosity we speak of comes from a deep desire to understand, a capacity to engage, and a willingness to shift fundamental beliefs. When we allow ourselves to enter this arena, we experience deep curiosity. In deep curiosity we feel driven to get to know others better, to truly understand where they are coming from and what they can offer to the problem at hand. Deep curiosity is a willingness to hang in there, to seek the gem in another's point of view, even if we don't like the person.

Curiosity keeps our minds open and helps us see the world in its complexity and wonder. Having an attitude of curiosity puts us in a state of Gracious Space because we look through a lens of interest, not judgment.

Curious George and Alice in Wonderland are great fictional icons of curiosity – they were always getting into things and having adventures. Children are naturally curious, asking how and why things happen the way they do. Scientists, journalists and doctors are paid to be curious, asking questions and figuring things out.

But over time our curious edge, even for those who are curious for a living, can start to fade. We get busy and stop taking adventures of the mind. As we mature we are encouraged to form opinions about who we are and what we believe. Once we do this, it is difficult to stop and reconsider. The train of opinion leaves the station, pulling away from other possibilities. We proceed through life as if we've got it figured out, because we do, in part. But if we believe we've got it *all* figured out, *all* the time, we lose our ability to be curious. We may even start to think people who ask questions are ignorant or lazy, or that curious people are nosy busybodies. Curiosity can get a bad reputation.

Fortunately, being curious is like riding a bike. We can always get back on even if we haven't tried it for a long time. So what would happen if we brought more curiosity into our lives? What would happen if we asked "why" more often? What if when faced with a new idea or person, we reacted with genuine interest, playful puzzlement, and followed where it led? Allowing ourselves a childlike sense of wonder will open new possibilities and yield surprising results. Curious George is always smiling at the end of his adventures.

Curiosity has ripple effects. When we carry a spirit of curiosity, we cause other people to be inquisitive with us. We make it okay that neither knows the answer – we can explore the future together as if setting off on a great adventure.

The spirit of Gracious Space is nurtured by practicing intention, compassion and curiosity. From here, we can express Gracious Space externally.

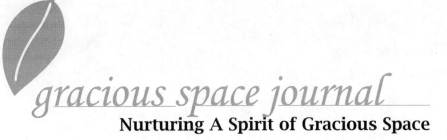

gracious space journal
Nurturing A Spirit of Gracious Space

1.   *What is my source of grace? How do I nurture this source?*

2.   *How will I remain gracious when others are uncooperative or apathetic?*

3.   *How do I express compassion toward others?*

4.   *How curious am I? How do I express my curiosity?*

5.   *How much do I allow others to be curious about me and my ideas?*

a setting that is expressed externally

"Leadership is practiced not so much in words as in attitude and in actions."

— *Harold Geneen*

Create a gracious physical setting

The external expression of Gracious Space is an environment that fosters courageous and honest conversation. It is a setting where people feel welcome and comfortable. Expressing Gracious Space externally means altering the physical environment and interactions with others to unleash creativity, encourage learning and deepen relationships. We may even have more fun!

An outer expression of Gracious Space can mean simple hospitality, such as providing drinks and snacks. We create a gracious physical environment when we attend to basic human necessities: by ensuring everyone can see the presenter or the displays; knows when the breaks are and where the restrooms are; knows the rules about cell phones; and clearly understands how to participate. It can mean affirming someone's special effort or success in public, perhaps at a staff meeting. These basic considerations go a long way toward helping people feel involved, confident, and ready to participate.

We can create a gracious physical setting with aesthetics, such as a floral arrangement, the use of fabric, art, colors, candles and music, or by increasing the natural light or rearranging the furniture. One woman at Seattle Public Utilities said all she did was remove the pile of reports from the guest chair in her office. "People can sit down when they meet with me, and now all my conversations are better," she said.

Cathy Capers deals with tense situations at work and noticed that she couldn't relax at the office. She redecorated her bedroom at home to create a soothing environment where she could renew herself at the end of the day. Then she collected toys and placed them around her office to encourage play and relaxation. She initiated an ice cream social among her colleagues, and found that food and laughing helped lessen their suspicions and heighten their interest in each other. "As

I created more Gracious Space in my personal life, it was easier to encourage it in the office," Cathy said.

Giving Gracious Space a physical dimension can be fun. All it takes is some attention and time. When the physical environment is inviting, we can turn our attention to the second part of the outer life of Gracious Space: fostering interactions that deepen the dialogue and encourage respect for conflicting ideas.

Attend to interactions with others

It can be helpful to start with an awareness of our current interactions. Do we feel rushed in our conversations? Are we multi-taskers who might be perceived as unapproachable? Are we honestly interested in what others think?

"When I developed an internal Peer Support Team I arranged my office so others would feel welcome," said Trisha King Stargel, former training coordinator for the Kent Police Department in Washington. "I wanted them to feel safe. Several people remarked on how comfortable they felt. Some of this was the environment; some was the caring I projected. It is incredibly important to not only pay attention to the external environment, but how we as humans impose our humanness onto others." Trisha discovered that her personal *attention* to others and her *intention* for them, created a more gracious feeling between them. Our attention and intention can create an environment where people feel comfortable talking about difficult or personal issues. When we assume good intent, others will respond. Just like the adage, "If you put a crown over their heads they will become kings and queens," we help them be their best.

This may not come naturally, especially if we have historical tension with someone. It doesn't do much good to create an inviting atmosphere and just sit back and hope they catch on. We need to introduce people to the new environment, describe what we are trying to accomplish, and how they can participate or help.

Perhaps we start by smiling. Or we can introduce the term "Gracious Space" and ask people to talk about what it means to them. We can incorporate their definitions into group norms and how they agree to treat each other. Adopting Gracious Space as a way to be together is an uplifting decision on many levels. Group members recognize they are more capable with grace, curiosity, and compassion in their midst. They may sigh at their definitions of Gracious Space and say, "Isn't this nice?"

Over time we may notice that the spirit and setting begin to influence each other. The inner spirit and attitude of Gracious Space is reflected in what we do, say, and create externally. The gracious physical spaces and our intentional interactions with others reaffirm who we are inside. This reciprocal influence strengthens and affirms the behaviors and skills of Gracious Space.

Cultivating an internal spirit and external expression for Gracious Space creates a foundation for effective and ethical leadership. In Gracious Space, people feel welcome and encouraged to learn. In the next section we will explore the two commitments of Gracious Space: "invite the stranger" and "embrace learning in public."

the spirit and the setting influence each other

The mutual influence of the spirit and setting of Gracious Space is demonstrated at Seattle Public Utilities, a 1,400-person agency that oversees the city's water, solid waste and sewer systems. Employees were introduced to Gracious Space as part of an advanced leadership program that the Center helped design and deliver. The utility adopted Gracious Space as a fundamental capacity for employees and leaders. Participants say that Gracious Space has been one of the most evocative elements of the program, both personally and professionally. They report being more gracious with themselves, and being more comfortable asking for help, taking risks, and mentoring each other. Over the four years of the program, the culture at SPU has become more open, positive and productive. The entire organization is a stronger learning community. Over time, the staff has discovered that the dimensions of spirit and setting catalyze each other.

"Gracious Space is the foundation of all our leadership development work," said Joanne Peterson, director of Human Resources and manager of the Directions program.

gracious space journal

Create a Gracious Space Setting

1. *What does a gracious setting look and feel like to me?*

2. *What items can create a physical environment that feels more gracious for myself and others? (In the office, at home, etc.)*

3. *In what ways do I interact with others that are intentional and positive?*

4. *In what ways do I interact with others that could undermine my desire to create Gracious Space?*

5. *How can I be more intentional in my interactions with others? How can I express myself and my desires in a more welcoming manner?*

6. *How will I start my next meeting in a way that reflects a more gracious setting?*

a commitment to invite the stranger

"Leadership has a harder job to do than just choose sides. It must bring sides together."

— *Jesse Jackson*

The Center defines Gracious Space as a spirit and a setting where we "invite the stranger" and where we "embrace learning in public." We invite the "stranger" because we need diverse perspectives to see the whole picture and gain clarity. We learn in public when we truly listen to a new thought or a conflicting idea and are open to changing our minds. This next section shows how these two commitments can create a space that is unique and valuable in today's fast-paced world.

Invite the "Stranger"

For our purposes in describing Gracious Space, the concept of the "stranger" represents diversity, and the word "strangeness" represents something intriguing and different to be explored. The Center for Ethical Leadership believes we have much to gain by moving closer to that which we do not understand. We use the term "stranger" lightly and with a positive connotation. We do not wish to erect false or negative barriers between us and others who appear to be different. Rather, we believe that special attention must be given to those who disagree or think differently, so that we can truly explore wide-ranging alternatives. This is especially true when working with any dimension of the common good. The more inclusive we are in our understanding of the common good, the more progress we can make.

Many people have initial difficulty being with others who are different. Our society tends to congregate like-minded individuals. Neighborhoods are segregated not by law but by our degree of comfort; friendships form among people with whom we share interests. Despite our tendency to stay within a comfort zone of familiarity, diversity has a way of creeping in. Nature abhors a monoculture, and ultimately will find ways to mix us up with one another.

Author and scholar Parker Palmer noticed this tendency of diversity finding a way in, and determined that two rules apply to human communities. The first rule is: the last person in the world you want to show up, shows up. The second rule is: as soon as you get that person to leave, someone else comes to take his or her place. It appears futile to try to gather only the people you like or agree with. Because of this "Murphy's Law" of community, Palmer concludes, "Community is dependent upon our willingness to invite the stranger."

Today we seem to have an abundance of communities: the business community, the academic and scientific communities, the gay and lesbian community, and a myriad of ethnic communities. We bestow the label of "community" on any group of individuals that has something in common. Palmer would say these are not true communities because they do not include the "stranger." They are based on commonality, and so perhaps they should be called clubs. A true community is where we encounter people different from ourselves. It is found at the grocery store or the public park. We can invite "the stranger" into our lives or work. The "stranger" is someone who thinks differently, acts differently or has a different background. They have "strange" ideas and "strange" customs, and could be very interesting people to have around.

When the "stranger's" perspective is most valuable

Gracious Space assumes it is beneficial to broaden our thinking and increase our options before acting. The approach of "inviting the stranger" is therefore most appropriate for those of us who tend to make decisions quickly and in isolation. We live in a society with a strong bias for action, sometimes at any cost. Many of us grew up hearing the admonition: *don't just stand there, do something!* In times of stress, we often default to doing something even if it is wrong, premature, or ill-conceived. When faced with a decision we often feel pressure to move quickly to solution. Gracious Space offers a framework for slowing down and considering diverse opinion, *before* we take action.

Ron Heifitz, author of <u>Leadership Without Easy Answers</u>, offers a two-part test to determine when we need to invite "the stranger." When faced with a complex situation, he advises that we first ask:

- Is there a single authority or institution that can handle this situation? If the answer is no, then we need the help of other people. We then need to ask:

- Does the work require a change in attitude, beliefs, assumptions or behavior? If the answer is yes, we need more than one perspective to move forward.

It is as if we each hold a piece of the puzzle. In order to complete the puzzle and resolve the issue, everyone needs to bring their piece. Not only will diverse perspectives help complete the puzzle, they can generate a breakthrough situation – one where a creative solution emerges from sharing different ideas. The greater the difference in thinking, the more creative the solution will likely be.

While many of us have an innate drive for closure, others are reluctant to make a final decision. They want more data and want to keep their options open. Keeping an open mind comes easily; coming to closure does not. For these people, inviting the "stranger" comes naturally. In times of stress, they default to more process and information. There comes a time, however, when more information is not helpful or needed. Gracious Space is not an open ticket for endless process with no closure. Gracious Space does not advocate for *more* process, but for *better* process. Leaders need to develop a sense of when enough discussion is enough, and help others understand the criteria and timelines for making a decision.

Our action-oriented culture and busy organizations tend to minimize opportunities to invite "the stranger" and share diverse opinion. Yet in nature, diversity is insurance for life. A diverse ecosystem has been shown to be more resilient to disease and healthier over the long term. Scientists have shown that the same is true for humans. Genetically, individuals who marry outside the family have healthier babies; those that intermarry are often prone to physical and neurological problems. Many cultures forbid marriage among family members because of this phenomenon. Socially, the fields of Leadership and Organizational Development have put forth many books and articles describing how a group is typically more creative, more productive and more immune to setbacks than an individual. Most of us know from experience that many ideas yield better results, yet it still can be difficult to do.

Move beyond tolerance of differences

For some, diversity is something to be tolerated. Dealing with people who are different – whether older, younger, from a different gender, profession or race - is time consuming and fraught with hidden ways to hurt someone's feelings. Inviting "the stranger" can feel like walking through a mine field.

Ervin Laszlo encourages us to think about diversity as "inter-existence," where we move beyond tolerance of differences to engage actively with each other. "Inter-existence denotes an active, mutually constitutive relationship, instead of a passive, purely external one," he writes. "It means that individuals, societies, enterprises and entire cultures exist not merely side by side, but *with* and *through* one another." Laszlo says that individuals who truly appreciate diversity will immerse themselves in relationships and strive to learn with and through others. Peggy Tabor Millin's poem below demonstrates this type of inter-existence:

> *Two separate raindrops on the window*
> *pushed by the wind,*
> *merged into one for a moment*
> *and then divided again,*
> *each carrying with it a part of the other.*
> *We never touch people so lightly that we do not leave a trace.*

Inter-existence is essential to Gracious Space. If we approach diversity as something to put up with, we will not create authentic Gracious Space, either in spirit or setting. We will miss opportunities for creative solutions and ultimately we will create a club, not a community.

If, on the other hand, we believe diversity is critical to a healthy organization or group, and necessary to resolve complex issues, we will go out of our way to invite the "stranger." Ultimately, if we all agree on the approach and the answer, all but one of us can go home. The "strangers" bring diverse perspectives to broaden our understanding and our possibilities. Think of it as an inexpensive way to get smarter.

The leader's role is to seek out those with diverse perspectives. If we listen to Parker Palmer, we would invite the last person we would ever want there. This could be someone who challenges our assumptions, thinks differently, or approaches the topic from a vastly different experience or knowledge base. We look for voices that are not represented. Who has something to say on the matter? Whose voice is traditionally absent or unwelcome? Who has a missing piece to the puzzle? Asking these questions and inviting the "stranger" will help us move toward greater creativity.

Discover and remove barriers

Inviting the "stranger" is a radical notion of diversity that may not succeed right away. A diverse gathering needs to be intentionally created and nurtured. If it were easy, we would do it on a regular basis without a second thought. But pressing deadlines and lack of resources often get in the way. We may be afraid of conflict or reluctant to consider an alternate point of view. We may believe that others cannot or will not comprehend the complexity of our issue or do not want to spend the time. These conditions are real barriers to inviting "the stranger."

If seeking diverse opinion is atypical for an organization, the employees or members within may initially be surprised and uncomfortable. They may be reluctant to speak up, fearful of retribution, or uncertain about the procedure. Leaders need to be clear about what we are asking of them. Leaders need to help people bring their gifts and perspectives to the conversation. We need to develop relationships and establish trust, especially for those people used to fighting to be heard, or being left out of the process altogether.

In his seminal work, <u>Servant Leadership</u>, Robert Greenleaf says the true mark of a servant leader is when people "grow in your midst." He calls it The Best Test: "Do those served grow as persons; do they, while being served, become healthier, wiser, freer, more autonomous, more likely themselves to become servants?"

When we call people into Gracious Space we invite them to learn about a specific issue, but also about themselves. We create space for their opinions and questions. We help them learn to work better with differences and see conflict as a positive, creative force rather than a destructive, painful inevitability. A leader's role is to create the environment where such learning and growth are possible.

Guidelines can help remove barriers to gathering a diverse group. A group can create guidelines for Gracious Space in as little as fifteen minutes. Start by asking them what Gracious Space means to them, and the characteristics it represents. Then create a list of guidelines they agree to pay attention to as they work together.

It is similar to inviting people to plant a beautiful garden. When asked what aspects of Gracious Space they want to bring into their midst, people name things like respect, honesty and humor. For many, these words are hopeful, as vibrant and promising as roses and peonies are in the garden. They create a colorful, inviting garden of Gracious Space they can't wait to be in. Once there, they don't want to leave. This leads us to the second commitment of Gracious Space - learning in public.

the confluence invites diversity

Every other year the Center for Ethical Leadership hosts an event called The Confluence, a gathering of diverse people to discuss a daunting and compelling social issue. Participants spend three days discussing the issue and catalyzing creative, collaborative action. When the Center recruits for the event, we make every effort to walk our talk about gathering diversity.

We brainstorm all the different people who have a role in the issue: business people, educators, government employees, ordained and lay religious representatives, human service professionals, students, the elderly, neighbors with different political leanings, people with varying income levels, genders, geographic locations, and so forth. We find out which segment of the population is most impacted, and invite several of those individuals.

The first two Confluence events in 1999 and 2000 addressed poverty and the increasing gap between rich and poor. Not only did we invite professionals charged with understanding and managing the economic vitality of the region, we invited homeless men and women, "working poor," youth, single parents, teachers, and others concerned for their financial future. Confluence organizers waived the conference fees for many participants, paid child-care and travel expenses and reimbursed them for time away from work. We discovered many barriers to convening a diverse gathering, and are still working to understand and remove them.

When it came to understanding the complex cycles of poverty – what keeps people in and what helps them get out – those with first-hand experience knew the most. They knew which policies and incentives worked and which did not. Their personal experience gave them a valuable perspective to share with those trying to fix the problem.

Shelia Proby, a single mother who spent two years homeless and many more struggling to support her five children, attended the first Confluence.

"The Confluence gave the opportunity for people to talk about important issues that don't normally get addressed," she said. "I didn't think so many people cared. You brought strangers together and created a strong bond. It was a very empowering experience."

When the Center invites people to the Confluence, we describe the perspectives we hope they will share. Many expect the Confluence to be like other conferences they have attended, but once they arrive and begin to work in Gracious Space, they realize something is different. As they become more comfortable, they begin to express themselves openly and start to share their other talents. Singers, artists, and comedians have surfaced from those who trusted the Gracious Space of the Confluence. Others leaders emerge as passionate youth with a hip-hop beat and people who think out of the box.

The Confluence strives to create a place where people feel welcome and safe to explore tough issues, and have the time to appreciate different ideas. We ask participants to select aspects of Gracious Space to live by for their three days together. These shared guidelines create an environment where participants can deeply listen to each others' experiences and points of view. If they forget, they remind each other in a graceful or humorous way.

"This group of diverse people was brought together and asked to share all their gifts and talents," said Seattle City Councilman Peter Steinbrueck. "This showing of the self inspired a deeper level of relationship than that which we get to see in the workplace. I feel much more connected to people I met at the Confluence than people I've met more frequently through other meetings."

gracious space journal
Invite the Stranger

1. *How do I respond when people think and act differently from me?*

2. *Do I tend to make decisions quickly and in isolation, or do I prefer to gather more data and keep options open? What is my default mode in times of stress?*

3. *What situations or problems am I involved in that cannot be solved by one person? What situations am I involved in that might require a shift in attitude or belief?*

4. *Who needs to be at the table to move forward on these situations? What diverse viewpoints could help? How do I decide when I have enough information to move forward?*

5. *What barriers might exist to inviting the "stranger" and gathering diverse perspectives?*

6. *How can I remove these barriers to create an inclusive and creative group?*

a commitment to learn in public

"An adult who ceases after youth to unlearn and relearn his facts and to reconsider his opinions...is a menace to a democratic community."

— *Edward Thorndike*

Edward Thorndike's quote above reminds us that learning is a lifelong process that improves ourselves and our society. Learning occurs when we unfreeze our certainty. Learning happens when we hear new information or another's truth and reconsider our own experiences and knowledge.

When groups engage in learning openly together, everyone comes out ahead. It is as if the group's shared intelligence leaps forward a notch. People see themselves as part of an "imagination infrastructure," building the capacity of many people to jointly conceive of solutions and a common future. Within this imagination infrastructure, we become aware of the fullness of the issue, grasp the value of each other's perspectives and view the diversity of possible solutions.

This is what the Center calls "learning in public." Learning in public is opening ourselves to diverse ideas and discussing them in Gracious Space with others with the intent to gain knowledge and understanding.

W. Edwards Deming once said, "Learning is not compulsory... neither is survival." Most of us today believe the world is becoming more complex and demanding. We get overwhelmed by everything we are expected to know, and it may seem our very survival is at stake. Learning in public is a tool for dealing with this complexity. When we learn in public we create a sense of sharing the burden and we may even find solace. Seeing the "stranger" as an ally, rather than an enemy, is central to dealing with complexity.

Up to this point, Gracious Space has asked a lot of us. Bringing compassion and a curious mind and inviting diverse people with "strange" ideas to the table is hard work for anyone. Now Gracious Space asks us to learn in public: to listen in a new way; to be willing to be influenced; to hold our opinions lightly; to admit we don't know; to be ready to change our minds.

The Richard Hugo House is a gathering place for writers in Seattle, Washington. It is also a place that embraces learning in public. Members and guests are encouraged to form groups to discuss books, written work, opinions and ideas. Frances McCue, founder and director, recalled a recent interaction in the halls of Hugo House that demonstrates the adventure of learning in public.

A young man dressed in a "Goth" style with baggy pants, spiked hair and pierced body parts, passed a distinguished-looking older gentleman in the entryway.

"What are you here for?" the young man asked.

"I'm writing a story on how my father died," replied the older man.

"Cool!" said the young man. "I'm into death, too." They walked upstairs together to talk about their shared interest.

Frances calls this moment a "collision of possibility." Two very different people, bumping into each other by chance, allowed something new to emerge from the chance encounter. They could have gone their separate ways, thinking the other too strange to bother with. But they were willing to be influenced by the other's story and formed an unexpected friendship. They were willing to see a "stranger" as an ally toward a common goal. They were willing to learn something, right there in the public hallway.

It is like sitting in a bumper car at the amusement park. We are vulnerable and open to "collisions of possibility." Some of us will be excited; some of us will be nervous or guarded. Some may hang back. We do not know what will come at us, or from which direction. Some will laugh the whole time. Some might get into an argument. Since we have invited "strange" people with different viewpoints and backgrounds, almost anything could happen.

The role of the leader is to hold the belief that each person has something valuable to contribute. Leaders hold the expectation that others will learn something about the issue, and will increase their capacity to act for a shared vision. When we hold this intention, the collisions of possibility become real opportunities and the group is transformed into a learning community.

Create a learning community

Peter Senge defines a learning community as any group that is more interested in alignment of purpose than agreement on process.

"Alignment means functioning as a whole," he writes. "Building alignment is about enhancing a team's capacity to think and act in new synergistic ways, with full coordination and a sense of unity because team members know each other's hearts and minds." For Senge, a learning organization is one that focuses more on the vision than on how things are done. A learning community occurs when a group of "strangers" is willing and able to integrate its thinking into a larger whole and a more plausible future, and create an imagination infrastructure.

Learning can be exhilarating. We can probably recall the moment we perfected a ski turn, or finally figured out a difficult math formula, or learned to play a favorite song on the piano or guitar. Remember the rush? We often feel euphoric when we learn. We are willing to wade through the awkward phase, trying again and again until we master the task we set out to learn. We are overjoyed when we succeed. This is true no matter how old we are. The ability to learn and grow keeps us alive and engaged.

But as with curiosity, we may stop learning as time passes. We may equate needing to learn something with an admission of ignorance. Sometimes admitting we do not know something is so painful we make something up or just keep quiet. As adults, we are expected to have answers, so we may hide our ignorance and avoid situations where we are unfamiliar. Try taking up skiing or piano or going back to school as an adult, and we quickly realize how much courage and commitment it takes to be continually, and publicly, outside our comfort zone. It is rare for adults to put themselves in settings where they are awkward and incompetent and everyone knows it.

Learning can be especially challenging for leaders who are expected to have answers. Not only do they have to admit they do not know what to do, they have to give up control and get input from others. Peter Senge describes the difficulties facing leaders in a learning community:

> *"As others become involved, the original leadership group typically experiences a crisis of diversity, in which they must either yield influence to other people with different styles, or see the*

effort's impact dwindle. The skills of team learning and dialogue
are vital at this stage, so that people can learn and lead together,
encompassing their varied perspectives."

Learning can be a challenging experience that requires humility and courage. We all go through the awkward, frustrating stage of
knowing we want to do something we have not yet mastered. It takes
humility to realize we do not know it all. It takes humility to let someone teach us. It takes courage to be open-minded and admit we were
wrong, or uninformed, or simply behind the times. It takes courage to
voice our perspectives and dreams.

So if learning is awkward and painful, why would we want to do
it in public? How awful to be "found out," or realize we do not know
something as well as we thought we did, while others are present. And
yet we do it; many of us crave it. Maybe we are willing to learn in public because we want to share the discovery process and the accomplish-
ment. Maybe we do it because we believe there are things we still need
and want to know, and realize this is something we do best in community. Maybe we learn in public because we are social creatures at
heart. To learn is to be fully alive and fully human. Learning in public
recognizes that the learning process is natural, and encourages us to
get over our fears so that we can work better together.

Ceylane Meyers, coordinator of the Buffalo Kellogg Leadership
for Community Change program, and Regional Director of the Public
Policy and Education Fund of New York, says learning in public has
helped her group work better together. "We have such a diverse group
that we come up against some real racial issues," she said. "The way
Buffalo has worked in the past is that people stay in their camps and
do not work together. We were afraid if we addressed the conflict, it
would disintegrate us. But learning in public says it is okay to disagree, and if we stay true to our values and what we have in common,
we can have honest discussions. The group created that space and was
able to move past feeling attacked into real collaboration for the community."

When we meet someone who believes differently, we can either
dismiss them and their difference, or move closer so that we can learn.
Moving closer is a courageous and humble step. While we may still
disagree after the conversation, we will have gained skill for learning
in public. We may be more in alignment over a vision or idea. We may
have clarified beliefs or gained respect for the other person because
of the authenticity of the exchange. We may even – *gasp!* – change our

minds. Gracious Space can make learning fun, and recognizes learning as an act of leadership.

It could help to enter Gracious Space as if going to a party at a friend's house. Attitudes of curiosity *(who will be there and what will they say?)* and compassion *(I'm sure these are nice people)* make learning in public more enjoyable. Gracious Space minimizes the shame and fear that can accompany admissions of confusion or ignorance. Gracious Space enables us to bring good intent and a desire to improve the organization or community. Gracious Space encourages us to learn together so we can do better work. Over time this becomes easier and more natural, and as Robert Greenleaf says, people will grow in the midst of our gracious leadership.

gracious space journal

Embrace Learning in Public

1. *How do I know when I have really learned something?*

2. *How important is it to figure things out for myself?*

3. *How do I react when others give me feedback on my ideas?*

4. *How do I offer feedback to others' ideas?*

5. *How comfortable am I with "not knowing?" How can I increase my comfort with learning in public?*

6. *Where do I want to have a learning community? What can I do to get that started?*

a container for working with conflict

"It is not best that we should all think alike; it is difference of opinion which makes horse races."

— *Mark Twain*

The benefits of Gracious Space are greatest when there is a need for a discussion of diverse opinion and/or when conflict is likely. Gracious Space can help in these situations by diffusing anxiety and fostering trust, and by creating ground rules and expectations for difficult, but ultimately productive, conversations.

Gracious Space is not a conflict-free setting. But when they first try to define Gracious Space, many people think automatically of safety and comfort. Gracious Space *does* provide safety and comfort, but it goes much further. Gracious Space is designed to hold conflict, not keep it out. In Gracious Space people bring compassion and curiosity and are encouraged to learn in public with people with "strange" ideas. This sets Gracious Space apart from an environment that is merely safe, polite or civil.

A group of neighborhood volunteers realized the difference between "civil" conversation and true Gracious Space when their project finished and the false civility crumbled. One member said that being too polite buried the conflict, and the nice, safe atmosphere actually blocked the core issues that needed attention.

"At the height of our work, we put our private interests and political relationships on the shelf. We were in a euphoric state, with so much good will it was extraordinary and inspiring. Moved by that spirit, the work proceeded quickly and well. We planned. We did analysis. We built community relationships. During this time, if someone came in who could not join in this heady experience, it was as if the group shooed them out.

"We should have watched for the hubris that comes from creating such a precious thing. If we had been more combative, more accepting of conflict, we would have built a stronger foundation. Once the process was done and the suspension of disbelief stopped,

> *all of the political realities, private interests and power dynamics entered in spades. The neighborhood lost its unity and is still struggling."*

Gracious Space does not shrink from controversy. In fact, due to the diversity gathered, we should expect conflict to be a natural part of the process. The more "strangers" we invite, the more diversity we will have, and the more differences of opinion will surface. The diagram below demonstrate how diversity leads to difference of opinion, which in turn will lead to conflict. The leader's job is to ensure that conflict leads to positive, creative results, rather than a negative and destructive situation.

Differences of opinion will lead to conflict. This is natural and desired. If conflict does not arise, there is probably one of two things happening. First, there may not be enough diversity in the room. Secondly, there may not be enough Gracious Space established; thus people will not be willing to speak up or disagree.

In either case, we risk "groupthink" when differences of opinion are absent. Groupthink is a concept identified by Irving Janis that refers to faulty decision-making in a group. Groups experiencing groupthink do not consider all alternatives and they desire unanimity at the expense of quality decisions. See the Appendix for the typical symptoms of groupthink and ways to avoid them.

A group that values a quick, simple agreement over a learning-oriented, divergent exploration will shield itself from conflict. Yet, we have seen that conflict is a normal part of the creative process. The role of the leader is to create a space gracious enough to contain and explore the conflict.

Explore conflict as a potential for creativity

According to Fred Kofman, three conditions must be present simultaneously for true conflict to exist. First, there must be disagreement about what to do or believe. Second, there must be a limiting factor that prevents the parties from pursuing more than one action. Something is scarce, such as time or resources. Third, there must be unclear property rights, or a lack of clarity over who has the power and authority to make the decision. These three conditions create a conflict.

For example, Kofman says, if a wife wants to take her next vacation in a quiet cottage by the sea, but her husband wants to go to a ski resort, they have the elements of conflict. They disagree on where to go. They cannot do both, as time, finances, and their desire to vacation together, are limiting factors. As a team, they usually make decisions together, so there is no clear authority figure in this disagreement.

This impasse can be broken with the tools of Gracious Space. By using inquiry and curiosity, they can uncover the underlying motivation for their positions. Perhaps the wife simply wants solitude, and a break from a busy schedule. The sea sounded nice, but she could also find solitude amidst some towering firs in a secluded mountain village. Perhaps the husband wants to have an active vacation, and skiing sounded like a good idea. He is willing to consider kayaking or beach hiking as an alternative. When they uncover their motivations, both parties discover room for common ground. They may decide on an entirely different, third alternative. Kofman and others have written extensively about how to negotiate conflicts in a creative, respectful way. See the Appendix for more resources on conflict resolution and negotiation.

The leader's job is to create the Gracious Space, explore the diverse opinions, and then steer the conflict toward a positive, creative direction. Without good leadership, differences of opinion often veer toward unfriendly exchanges and negative results. Many of us have experienced this, and consequently have learned to dislike and avoid conflict. It may help to remember that different does not equal bad. While difference can disintegrate into destructive disagreements, with good intent and Gracious Space, difference can sow the seeds of breakthrough creativity. Jagoda Perich-Anderson describes how creative conflict can transform into new, collaborative possibilities:

"Insights, inventions and innovations hardly ever come about when we are feeling satisfied and comfortable with the

status quo. They come from the energy created when there is a push, a need or a desire for something to be different – a tension between what is and what could be.

"Creative conflict is recognizable for its spirit of curiosity and mutual respect and its commitment to learning and finding the best solution or direction to take. When that is the case, interactions are characterized by questions and a lot of listening to try to get to know and understand (without necessarily having to agree with) the other points of view."

In the past we expected our leaders to have answers for our difficult issues and guide us wisely into the future. In simpler times, this approach may have worked. But today's complexities require many minds and many experiments. The single most important contribution of a good leader could be to ask the right questions of a diverse group of people – to invite the "stranger" and learn in public – and lead the way to consider conflicting opinions and find creative solutions.

gracious space journal
Guide Conflict Into Creative Solutions

1. *How comfortable am I with conflict? What is my first response when faced with disagreements, limiting factors and unclear authority?*

2. *What skills do I bring to situations of conflict?*

3. *How can I encourage others to welcome conflicting ideas, and be patient and courageous in the midst of conflict?*

4. *What situation could use some Gracious Space?*

Spirit:
   What role can compassion play in this situation? How can I approach from a place of curiosity and encourage the same from others?

Setting:
   How can I make the setting more comfortable for participants? What intention and attention could help shift the conversation into one that is less combative and more creative?

Invite the "stranger:"
   What other perspectives could help resolve this issue?

Learn in public:
   How open are we to learning with each other?

a tool to promote the common good

"Good, the more communicated, more abundant grows."

— *John Milton*

Introduction

We have described Gracious Space in the context of individuals, groups, organizations and communities. But Gracious Space has a role beyond our communities and organizations – it is a tool for advancing the common good.

The Center for Ethical Leadership was founded with the intention of empowering people to become transformational leaders and work for a more just society. That core mission spawned programs that invite participants to focus on a balance of individual and community needs. These programs seek to initiate change in service to the common good, and this work is greatly aided by Gracious Space.

What is the Common Good?

The common good can mean many things, and ultimately, we each need to choose our own definitions. It may help to know that in the past dozen years repetitive themes have emerged to define the common good. These themes include equity, fairness and the opportunity for every person to be clothed, fed, healthy, safe and free to achieve their potential. For many years, the Center's definition of the common good was: *liberty and justice for all, with an additional measure of mercy and compassion for the least fortunate and the most vulnerable among us.*

When we said "all," we meant all, including those who do not have a voice. The latter part of the definition is critical because over time, different groups of people in different settings or times are the least fortunate and the most vulnerable. In all cases when we care about those who are marginalized we, in the end, care about ourselves and the whole community.

The Center's definition of the common good has evolved to consider different forms of justice, including social, environmental and economic. We ask people to consider whether their definition of the common good is equitable, respects different needs while honoring the needs of the whole, and whether it promotes the public good or welfare. The Center now defines the common good as *fostering healthy, just and inclusive communities.*

Any robust definition of the common good will include our interconnectedness. Humans are social creatures who tend to gather in groups: families, tribes and clans. When the moment is right – floods, earthquake or a flat tire – humans have a habit of reaching out to strangers to offer aid, understanding that somehow we are all connected.

A friend of the Center tells a story of how her grandparents helped settle the state of Kansas. For the first two years the settlers lived in "soddies" – sod homes. At best, those homes must have been damp, dark and cold; yet they all chose to stay in their soddies until two wooden structures were built. Which two structures do you suppose those were? The church and the school.

Many of us will automatically know the answer to that question, not because we remember some obscure fact of history, but because the same sentiment and instinct that was in the hearts of those grandparents is present in our hearts too.

So why did they build the school and the church first? These structures represent an investment in their collective lives. Settlers understood the vulnerability of going it alone and knew that an investment in community was an investment in their own best future.

Deep down many of us realize that the good life involves not just goodness for our individual lives, but also for our lives together. In some deep way, we know we are connected to each other and that we will respond when the good life calls us beyond ourselves to attend to the concerns and interests of the community.

Seven Steps to the Common Good

1. Create Gracious Space

Gracious Space is central to the Center's work because it provides a context for exploring the common good. In Gracious Space, we can look at the current situation and ask ourselves: "Who is most vulnerable today?" "Who is the least fortunate?" "How do we foster healthy, just and inclusive communities?" Gracious Space brings all voices into the discussion. It provides an environment for the hard work of examining the policies, systems and realities that threaten or withhold the good for some of our citizens.

A commitment to the common good is noble and necessary work, but promoting it is difficult. People have different ideas about what "good" looks like and how it should be put into practice. Leaders and citizens who seek to transform organizations and communities need "safety zones" where they can explore difficult issues and imagine new futures. Gracious Space can be that zone, enabling us to discover new pathways, make new choices, and adopt new behaviors and habits in our communities and institutions.

Gracious Space plays an essential role on a journey to the common good, because, without the graciousness in which to question and learn, we will likely conceive a more narrow interpretation of the common good. Without a spirit of compassion and curiosity, we may lack the trust and the will to commit to the remainder of the journey. In Gracious Space, we can join with others to search for shared solutions to society's problems.

As part of the research and development for our original leadership development models and programs the Center named seven steps for leadership and action on behalf of the common good. 1) Create Gracious Space; 2) Gather diverse people; 3) Critique the status quo; 4) Advance systems thinking and transformational and transforming change; 5) Promote ethical leadership and knowledge of core values; 6) Foster integrity and moral courage; and 7) Recall hope.

The following is an overview of steps two through seven, and how each of them contributes to the common good.

2. Gather Diverse People

What do we mean by diverse people? Certainly we include people from a different gender, race, ethnicity, socio-economic status, religious affiliation and sexual orientation than our own. During the last several years, we have also noticed that we are often divided by neighborhood, experience and profession. Business leaders usually congregate with other business leaders, and religious leaders often cluster among their peers. The same is true in government, philanthropy, media, education, and the blue-collar sector. We spend most of our waking hours with like-minded colleagues in vocational silos.

At first glance, Gracious Space could easily be misperceived as a vehicle for creating an emotionally antiseptic setting that seeks to avoid conflict. In fact, Gracious Space is at its most powerful and useful when difference or conflict is present, such as when diverse people come together.

Dr. Martin Luther King, Jr. said, "Peace is not the absence of tension but the presence of justice." When we gather diverse people in Gracious Space, it is to establish justice, trusting that real peace is a byproduct of an authentically just climate. In that gathering we may experience conflict. The good news is that conflict, when held in Gracious Space, creates an enlightened experience of dissenting views which can yield powerful results for the good.

Some of the divisions noted above are benign, and it is simply good practice for us to step out of our silos or comfort zones and see things from different points of view. Other divisions are not so benign, and are evidence of a lack of justice in our communities. Regarding the more egregious differences, the common good asks us to gather diverse people so we can wrestle with the injustices in our midst.

For instance, a diverse community might gather to address the racial disparities in achievement in K-12 education. Instead of blaming individuals or certain racial groups, the community acknowledges that this is a shared problem, and must be addressed collectively to solve it. Through the strength of their collective wisdom, voice and power, change for the common good is much more likely to occur.

If we sincerely hope to be promoters and creators of the common good, we must make every attempt to gather representatives of the community in its entirety.

3. Critique the Status Quo

Once we have gathered diversity, leaders or citizens who desire to advance the common good are obliged to critique the status quo. Offering critique should not be done lightly as it can unexpectedly and unnecessarily do harm. Words carry great weight. Words can lift up and transform or they can scar and disable. The art of critique requires a skilled balancing act between care and truth telling.

Sometimes we criticize someone – a child, athlete, friend or staff member – to help them become their best, in which case critique is intended as a gift. Other times we might criticize these people in order to do harm, feel right or superior, in which case our critique is more like a weapon. Before we offer a critique we need to check our intentions. If we are offering a gift, bring it; if we are brandishing a weapon, stow it.

A critique of the status quo is no different. We must do so in a way that is effective and does not do more harm than good. Simply complaining about the way things are is highly unlikely to advance the common good. Citizens and leaders need to ask: How and where is the system causing harm to others? Knowledge of these harmful patterns must then be articulated in public.

Once an injustice is named, we can create a moral agenda for social change. Furthermore, the common good asks us to do this challenging work with compassion – to speak the truth, in love, to power. Speaking the truth in love to power is a tricky balancing act that seeks justice for those who are oppressed while seeking to do no harm to the oppressor. The non-violent tactics of Mohandas Gandhi and Dr. King are clear examples of how love in action presents a compelling vision of the truth in a way that advances progress for the common good without perpetuating harm to those in power.

Before offering a critique, it is helpful to remember dimensions of our personal lives that still need fixing. When we get in touch with our own ongoing imperfections, we can deliver tough-love messages with greater gentleness and less self-righteousness, and increase the chances that our message will be heard. We need to remember that even an artfully worded critique spoken in love is rarely experienced as love by those who defend the status quo. Yet, if critique emerges from a place of personal integrity, and our intentions align with the common good, then critique must be delivered. Justice demands it of us.

We should also realize that the system we are about to critique is likely another generation's contribution to the common good. For example, the U. S. national highway system could be viewed, from the perspective of today's "green" consciousness, as an unwise use of fossil fuels. From today's vantage point, investing in fuel-efficient networks of high speed trains, local light rail and linked buses might seem like wiser choices. Yet, when the highway system was put in place the goal was to advance interstate commerce and provide the quick movement of materials and machinery necessary for national defense and livelihoods. What is currently seen as unwise was at one time a creative solution. This is true in other realms: that which appears unfair or ill-advised could in fact be part of an earlier revolution for freedom or justice.

4. Advance Systems Thinking and Transformational and Trans-forming Change

When we gather diverse people in Gracious Space and critique the status quo, we begin to see things we hadn't seen before. A systems analysis aids us in understanding the complexity of the system we are seeking to change. At the Center for Ethical Leadership, we are interested in using systems thinking to advance change for the common good.

Systems thinking is "a discipline for seeing wholes, recognizing patterns and interrelationships, and learning how to structure those interrelationships in more effective, efficient ways." Admittedly, trying to understand anything as a whole is difficult. Tackling something whole scale, such as how to transform a struggling school, or how to grow the perfect tomato, can be a complicated and mind-boggling task.

Some people spend their entire lives trying to understand the tomato. There is nothing like a fresh garden tomato, but tomatoes are notoriously difficult to grow, especially in cooler climates. A good tomato needs the right systems in place in order to develop into that masterpiece. Tomatoes need good sun and plenty of water, but not directly applied to roots. If blight occurs, the sickness is not just in the plant, but also in the soil. Even a hardy plant placed in diseased soil will develop the same blight and die.

Similarly, a child's education requires good schools, gifted and passionate teachers, and a child ready to learn. Education also is dependent upon a home free from harm, with adult role models who support the child's education through direct involvement. If educational reform leaves out any of these factors, or those of class size, peer culture, class and racial equity, and learning styles, reform will fall short. Systems analysis therefore takes a commitment to examine the whole.

The process of seeing the whole is the same in both examples. They begin with loving tomatoes and loving kids. If we are going to wholly understand anything, it is best to begin with great passion and compassion. Systems analysis thus requires a disciplined exploration based on deep, authentic interest.

Systems thinking also requires that we notice patterns and inter-relationships, causes and effects, which demonstrate the complexity of the system we are seeking to change. Using the school example, we would observe the patterns between parents, the teacher's union, government officials, children and teachers, and notice which patterns were helpful or get in the way of success. This deeper, richer under-standing provides a clearer perch from which we can choose more robust strategic directions for reform and re-creation.

Two models of leadership offer effective strategies for change that align with the common good: transformational leadership and transforming leadership.

We define transformational leadership as "changing the status quo for the common good." This type of leadership questions "busi-ness as usual" and seeks to advance systemic change for the benefit of the least fortunate and the most vulnerable. For example, in their transformational change efforts, civil rights leaders have changed bus ridership rules, school admission policies, and state and federal laws. Other transformational leadership examples include recent no smok-ing policies in restaurants and other public spaces, Child Labor Laws, Maternity and Paternity Leave policies and affirmative action.

Transforming leadership has the same end goal – the common good – but a different focus. The focal point of the transforming lead-er is not the status quo itself but the philosophical assumptions of the status quo. It does not seek to transform systems and institutions, but rather the hearts, minds and spirit of those who created the systems in the first place, or who are currently stewards and users of them.

By focusing on hearts, minds and spirits, transforming leaders seek to raise the awareness and behavior of individuals and institu-tions to higher levels of motivation and morality. When President Kennedy said, "Ask not what your country can do for you, ask what you can do for your country," he touched the hearts of a generation of Americans. Who knows how many people entered public service, joined the Peace Corps, or simply became more involved in their local community as a result of Kennedy's transforming vision? Other hearts, minds and spirits were touched by the transforming leadership efforts of Rachel Carson, whose 1962 book *Silent Spring* raised the sensibili-ties of many relative to environmental stewardship. In the same vein, Harriett Beecher Stowe's *Uncle Tom's Cabin*, published in 1873, raised moral awareness about the injustices of slavery.

Transforming leadership does not require speech-making or book-writing. It can simply be the result of inspired action in the world. Through her faithful service and daily compassionate action for the poorest of the poor in India, Mother Teresa inspired a shift in the hearts of many people worldwide, who then focused their service toward the needy in their own communities.

Transformational and transforming leaders are similar in their desire for justice and new visions for the common good, but they differ in substance and approach. Transformational leaders seek to change systems and institutions through acts, laws and policies because these public tools create more accountability. Transforming leaders intend to move a person to a differently principled view of life or a given situation, trusting that change is more lasting when it is written on someone's heart rather than just on the books. The common good requires both types of leadership.

5. Promote Ethical Leadership and Knowledge of Core Values

Ethical leadership is the essential combination of transformational and transforming leadership. Transformational leadership without a transforming strategy can lead to changes in the system but not the hearts, and the old problem is likely to simply resurrect in a new form. Cornel West, an American philosopher, author, and civil rights activist, said that because we have not adequately transformed hearts about racism, the racist systems of the 1950s in America have reappeared today in subtler forms as Jim Crow, Junior.

Conversely, engaging in transforming leadership without a transformational change agenda can easily be reduced to great prose in search of reality. What good are the most inspiring words if nothing actually changes for the good? Transforming words ring hollow in the ears of those who suffer here and now. The common good asks leaders for a two-fold commitment to change hearts and change systems, because then the possibility of moving towards the common good with sustainable results increases dramatically.

As ethical leaders seek the common good, they usually begin with a highly personal act – the awareness of and commitment to their own core values. James Fenhagen defines core values as:

"Values are more than ideals or moral absolutes to which we aspire. A value is an inner construct blending religious beliefs, ethical principles, societal norms and life experiences in a way

that empowers us to act. Everything we do – be it decisions we make or actions we take in the course of a day – is based on some consciously or unconsciously held value. Values are freely held and important enough to cause us to want to act on their behalf. One of the things that makes me unique is the particular value structure that empowers my life. There are elements I may hold in common with others but the particular combination is mine – It is values that create and maintain our lifestyle."

Our core values are or can become our core identity, our core intentions, and our core mission in life. In a hectic world where we can easily forget who we are, why we are here and what we would like to do with our lives, our core values remind us of the deepest understanding of our life's meaning and purpose.

It is helpful for leaders to have a practice which reminds us of core values each morning. Yet even with good intentions, we may discover that sometime before noon we do something to dishonor our values. When this happens, it should not be an occasion for guilt or shame; rather, it is an opportunity for awareness and action. It is an opportunity to give Gracious Space to ourselves.

As we grow in our commitment to our core values, we will experience more and more moments when we honor our values and live them well. When we do, we should celebrate. Give ourselves a moral pat on the back. Drink in the good taste of integrity and give thanks for it. Moments of celebration and gratitude help us stay on track, and over time, if we stay committed to our values they will become a vital part of our lives.

(The Center for Ethical Leadership has published a Core Values Exercise on its website for individuals and groups to discern their core values. We invite you to use this tool with your groups to move forward together with greater intention about your values.)

6. Foster Integrity and Moral Courage

As we integrate our values into our daily lives for the sake of the common good, we find ourselves in the territory of integrity and courage. "Integrity" shares a Latin root with the word "integer." An integer is a whole number, not divided or fractionalized, and the word integrity points to the same wholeness. Another definition of integrity comes from the textile industry. If a garment is woven from one end to the other without a seam, then is the garment said to have integrity.

Our lives could be seamless garments if we commit to our values in all facets of our lives. Integrity invites us to stand up for our values when it is easy and when it is hard. When our personal, professional, and civic lives are informed by the same core values, we become the beneficiaries of seamless lives dedicated to clear moral propositions. Integrity becomes a gift to ourselves.

As we move more deeply into a life of integrity we will naturally call those around us, both individuals and institutions, to seek the same. Integrity is infectious and one person's commitment to integrity can move a whole institution or community to follow suit.

It also takes moral courage to gather diverse people, critique the status quo, and advance change for the common good. Courage is not fearlessness – rather it is an inner quality that enables us to move into the challenges of the common good in spite of our fears.

Courage is derived from the French word "coeur," which means heart. When a person commits to their passionate concerns for the world, that heartfelt commitment will help him or her move into coura-geous leadership.

Courage comes in different forms. Physical courage is necessary to become an Olympic gymnast; psychological courage is necessary to fly solo in an airplane. Yet, the form of courage most essential for leaders who aspire to advance the common good is moral courage. Moral courage is the willingness and ability to align our actions with the call of our values and the demands of conscience. Ernest Heming-way underscores the unique nature of moral courage by reminding us that:

> *"Few people are willing to brave the disapproval of their fel-lows, the censure of their colleagues, the wrath of their society. Moral Courage is a rarer commodity than bravery in battle or great intelligence. Yet it is the one essential vital quality of those who seek to change a world, which yields most painfully to change."*

Moral courage is a willingness to do the right thing when the wrong thing is easier and less costly. Moral courage is the willingness to inquire, "What do my highest values ask of me in this situation?" This is neces-sary for all those who seek lives of integrity.

There are many sources of courage; here we will note four sig-nificant sources leaders can draw from: experience, values, community and spirituality.

Experience is a source of courage because as Eleanor Roosevelt said, "We gain strength, and courage, and confidence by each experience in which we really stop to look fear in the face ... We must do that which we think we cannot." Many of us have experiences that required us to act courageously, stand up for what we believed in, take actions of which we were uncertain. When faced with moral dilemmas of the common good, we can draw on this previous experience to more confidently face the current crisis.

Our values are a source of courage because they guide us to do the right thing. When we give ourselves to our values, they give back to us. If we commit to the value of wisdom we will, over time, find ourselves becoming wiser. When we commit to truth, we become more truthful ourselves. And when we commit to courageousness, we will find ourselves becoming more accustomed to acting with courage.

Community is a third source of moral courage, because here is the connection with others or to a cause that is greater than ourselves. With others we feel greater solidarity and strength to persevere when it might be easier to quit. The struggle for women's suffrage, civil rights and the rights of gay and lesbians are all housed in social movements. When we walk and make signs together, or nonviolently go to jail together, a bond forms. We find within ourselves a new resolve for enduring the hardships of making social progress for the common good.

Spirituality is a fourth powerful source of moral courage. Spirituality can be understood as the practice of transcendent relationships with the spiritual realm. Many leaders have leaned on and drawn from spirituality in their work, including Dr. King, Desmond Tutu, Lech Walesa (founder of the Polish Solidarity Movement), and Harriet Tubman (the "Moses" of her people). Whether in a Native American long house, Buddhist temple, synagogue, church, mosque or just outdoors, the spiritual realm is accessible to us. It is rarely experienced with our five senses, yet is felt nonetheless. Regardless of the tradition, the goal of spiritual practice is to prepare us to respond to life with greater presence, resolve and courage.

It takes courage to create Gracious Space, gather diverse people, critique the status quo, advance systems thinking and transformational and transforming change, and promote ethical leadership and values-oriented behavior. Courage infuses these leadership activities with the decisive actions necessary to advance the common good.

7. Recall Hope.

A leader's responsibility doesn't end with simply pointing out what needs to be changed, or addressing the systemic changes needed or the ways in which hearts and minds need to shift. Leaders need to point towards hope that change can and will occur. Hope is the final step of the Seven Steps to the Common Good, because hope can be the force that makes or breaks a change effort. Leaders must find hope within themselves and inspire others to find hope.

Asking a person to inspire hope is a lot like asking them to create fire. It can be done, but only with the right ingredients. To make fire, the right ingredients would be fuel, oxygen and a source of ignition. The three ingredients for hope are conviction, love and a transcendent vision.

Conviction tells us to commit to the common good even if our efforts appear fruitless or foolish. Conviction encourages the leader to continue to labor for the good trusting that hope – and change – will arrive. Conviction kept Nelson Mandela's hope alive while he endured nearly 28 years of imprisonment on Robben Island. His conviction for a just South Africa led him to the day when, against all odds, he was freed and elected President of his country.

Love is the second ingredient of inspiring hope. When we listen to our hearts, we remember who and what we love, and that we are loved. In our stillness we recall the faces, voices and stories of people who are suffering within the status quo. A leader's love for those who are disenfranchised and for the possibility of a brighter future can keep them hopeful and moving forward even in the darkest days.

The third ingredient of hope is a transcendent vision. Hope is not bound by present realities, rather, hope transcends present reality and grants a view of the future that neither rhyme nor reason can support. As Joan Chittister so eloquently says:

> *"When tragedy strikes, when trouble comes, when life disappoints us, we stand at the crossroads between hope and despair, torn and hurting. Despair cements us in the present; hope sends us dancing around dark corners trusting in a tomorrow we cannot see."*

Hope is fueled by the leader's conviction, by love and by a transcendent vision, but in the final analysis hope is not earned, it is bestowed. Hope is gifted upon leaders whose courageous steps move them into the difficulties of the day in pursuit of the common good. Emily Dickinson points to the idea of hope as a gift in her famous poem:

"Hope" is the thing with feathers –
That perches in the soul –
And sings the tune without the words –
And never stops – at all –

And sweetest – in the Gale – is heard –
And sore must be the storm –
That could abash the little Bird
That kept so many warm –

I've heard it in the chilliest land –
And on the strangest Sea –
Yet, never, in Extremity,
It asked a crumb – of Me.

"Yet never... asked a crumb..." In the poem there is no quid pro quo; hope is offered freely. Who or what then is the giver of this hope? "Hope perches in the soul," Dickinson writes. The soul is the home of Spirit. Spirit, then, is the giver of hope. Hope emerges from Spirit, and is a window to this realm, which existed before time and space. In this way, hope is pre-existent and eternal. It is the lasting nature of hope that accompanies us as we look the difficult truths in the eye, and seek life-giving choices and liberating futures.

If the road to the common good was paved and well-marked, there would be little need for hope. But history suggests the way to the common good is often filled with challenge and peril. A whole host of leaders can testify to the rocky nature of the road to the common good. The lives and struggles of Susan B. Anthony, Cora-zon Aquino and Frederick Douglass – to name only a few – suggest that the way to the common good sometimes requires leaders to climb up the rough side of the mountain. Leaders need conviction, love, and a transcendent vision to do their challenging work with hope. With hope the leader can move through the rocky terrain and find passage.

Gracious Space and the Common Good

The Seven Steps to the Common Good help leaders find their way to the common good. The seven steps serve as a tried-and-true pathway for leaders who find themselves in unfamiliar and unstable territory, and can provide a sense of what to expect and what is most needed in the midst of ambiguity or volatility.

When leaders find themselves in difficulty they can help themselves and others by creating Gracious Space, grounding themselves in their values, and recalling the promise of hope. When leaders find themselves capitulating to an unjust status quo they can fix their courage, and remember that leadership asks them to critique the status quo and advance systems thinking and change even when it is difficult.

These seven steps are an opportunity to develop seven habits of leadership. Habits are developed through daily practice. In an average day we can practice Gracious Space and live our values. We can engage in the critique and transformation of small things (e.g., starting a recycling program at work) as preparation for large-scale change opportunities that come our way. Integrity is welcome in any conversation and each day there are opportunities for courage. And which moment, group or gathering would not welcome a sincere offering of hope?

It is our belief that the most powerful place to begin the work of leadership for the common good is with the creation of Gracious Space. Gracious Space serves as the container in which the rest of the seven steps or habits can be practiced. Leadership often involves risk, and Gracious Space creates a setting in which leaders access the strength and support to risk leading on behalf of a better future.

Gracious Space also creates a setting where those being led are more likely to constructively engage the leader's actions and pursue the common good together. Gracious Space shifts the public space and the space in people's hearts and minds to create room for collective innovation and transformation.

Finally, Gracious Space transforms the pursuit into an experience of the common good itself. A friend of the Center once said, "You can't get to a good place in a bad way." This means that Gracious Space and the common good become one and the same. How we get there (the means) and the common good we envision (the ends) must be in alignment. When diverse people come together, welcome new ideas and perspectives, and ask questions that have the power to transform the good for all, the common good is made manifest.

As people sample a taste of the common good by working within Gracious Space, they become ready to transform the unjust systems and structures into new expressions of the common good. In this way, Gracious Space itself works as a harbinger of change and motivates people to manifest the common good in the realms where they live.

Closing

In Part I we explored the meaning and promise of Gracious Space. The benefits of cultivating a spirit, nurturing a setting, inviting diverse opinion of the stranger, and learning in public cannot be underestimated. The ripple effects of Gracious Space are subtle yet strong. Individuals, communities and organizations embracing Gracious Space have experienced profound changes in their relationships, conflicts, and change-related action. It doesn't much matter where we begin, just that we are committed. In Part II we will describe some tools and skills for creating Gracious Space.

gracious space journal

Advance the Common Good

1. *What is my definition of the common good?*

2. *Who is the "most vulnerable" or "least fortunate" in my community or organization?*

3. *What systems and policies promote the common good in my organization or my community?*

4. *What systems and policies might need to be changed to advance the good for more people?*

5. *How can Gracious Space help to advance the common good for my organization or community?*

part one review

- Gracious Space is a spirit and a setting where we invite the stranger and where we embrace learning in public.

- We all have innate abilities for Gracious Space. These need to be nurtured intentionally.

- The key to developing an inner life of Gracious Space is to tap into a source that is constant, personal, and immune to the ups and downs of others' moods.

- There are many simple things we can do to create a physical environment of Gracious Space.

- Inviting the "stranger" means we move beyond tolerance of diversity to being deeply curious and willing to hear others' truths.

- A community is a place where diversity occurs. A club is a place where people with shared interests find each other.

- Learning in public is challenging, exhilarating, and an excellent way to address complex issues.

- Gracious Space is most beneficial and powerful when conflicting ideas need to be discussed and difficult conversations need to be conducted.

- The existence of conflict in a diverse group is healthy and foreseeable. A leader's job is to direct the differences of opinion into positive, creative solutions.

part two:

creating gracious space

"Holes bored from opposite sides rarely meet."

— *Samoan proverb*

Gracious Space is born through compassion, curiosity, and a willingness to learn from others, but it is trust that enables Gracious Space to thrive. Trust gets people in the room, and keeps them there when the conversation gets difficult. Trust, listening and inquiry can transform individuals and groups. In Part II we explore some tools of building trust, listening, and inquiry that can help leaders create Gracious Space.

building trust

As we sit in the bumper car awaiting "collisions of possibility," we are no doubt trusting that the person we collide with will not hit too hard. We trust that their intent is similar to ours, and the rules of the game are understood. A basic level of trust is necessary for authentic learning and working together productively. Without trust we are cautious, suspicious and fearful. If we seek to empower others and transform organizations, our work must be animated by trust.

Bill Grace tells the following story about a friend's son to demonstrate the power of trust.

"Baylor is four years old. One Sunday after church he and I were playing in the fellowship hall. Baylor decided he wanted to fly. With enthusiasm he climbed on top of a folding table, crept toward the edge, and tumbled into my arms.

*"After that first successful run Baylor decided to test his limits.
He climbed again onto the folding table, stood at the far end and
ran its full length. When he reached the end he soared through
the air into my waiting arms. Baylor trusts me. Baylor trusts most
people."*

Bill's story about Baylor shows that trust is most easily measured by *what is possible when it is present.* A four-year old boy can fly because he trusts someone to catch him. Astounding things happen in the presence of trust: two people commit to a lifetime together; business leaders make deals over a handshake; parents send their children to schools. Trust can just as easily be measured by its absence. Without it, people withdraw, will not commit themselves, and will not take risks.

Dr. Oscar G. Mink, a respected psychologist and consultant specializing in executive leadership, defines trust as "a person's confident expectation that another person's behavior will be consistently responsive and supportive to the mutual interests of both persons." The people we trust act in predictable and competent ways that we come to rely upon. Think of some people we trust. What makes them worthy of our trust? How is their behavior responsive and supportive?

Now think about what makes us trustworthy. What can others rely upon – our behaviors, our knowledge, our abilities? By acting consistently in helpful ways, we build our trustworthiness. Stephen Covey calls this the "emotional bank account." By acting in a consistent and supportive manner over time, we make deposits into the trust account. Over time the deposits grow and we become trustworthy in the eyes of others. When this pattern stops, trust breaks down. If we get sloppy at work, are late picking up the kids, or start acting in unexpected and unsupportive ways, our colleagues, friends and family may lose the trust they had in our competence and character. We make withdrawals from the trust account.

Imagine what would happen if Bill made no effort to catch Baylor. The boy would fall to the ground. He would be scared and hurt. Would he do it again? He might forgive Bill once, and may even forget that he fell. But if he is dropped again, he will probably stop trusting that Bill will be there for him. He might start to doubt Bill about other things. He might extend his mistrust to other men or anyone in a church basement. Over time, Baylor would become a more cautious person.

The same cycle of trust is true with groups. In their research, Drs. Jack and Lorraine Gibb found that a beginning level of trust causes people to be more willing to share information. The more information they share, the more trust is developed among the members. As trust builds, members become willing to share even more information, creating a positive feedback loop. The increase of open information enables more effective goal setting and problem solving, which in turn increases the likelihood of productive and gratifying results. Therefore, they conclude, one proven way to increase trust is to share information. The diagram below demonstrates the Gibbs' trust cycle.

Trust can spread through a group like ripples on a pond. When one person demonstrates trust, others will respond. People feel freer to take risks and be creative. Like Baylor, we will take a chance to fly toward new possibilities, trusting we will land safely.

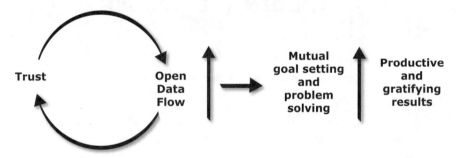

The Johari Window is an opening to build trust

The Johari Window, named after inventors Joseph Luft and Harry Ingham, is a useful model to describe the creation of trust between individuals or groups. A four-paned "window," as illustrated below, divides personal awareness into four different types: open, hidden, blind, and unknown. The lines dividing the four panes are like window shades which move as an interaction progresses. Trust is built by opening our windows to others, and by allowing others to open the windows to ourselves.

The window labeled "open" contains information *you know about yourself that others also know.* These are public aspects of ourselves, such as name, gender, skin color, approximate age, and an accent. It

The Johari Window

	Known to self	**Not known to self**
Known to others	OPEN	BLIND
Not known to others	HIDDEN	UNKNOWN

does not require a lot of trust to share these things. When we first meet a new person, this window is small because there has been little time to exchange information. As we get to know each other, the window opens downward, uncovering information that was hidden; or to the right as others give us feedback about our blind spots. As the "open" window grows larger and more information is shared, trust builds. With increased trust, our relationships are more open, we work better together, and we are willing to share more information.

The "hidden" window contains information *you know about your-self, but others do not.* There are many things about us that no one can tell just by looking. These include experiences, beliefs, hopes, fears or accomplishments. Family dynamics, other languages we speak, political views, hobbies, religious beliefs – essentially our whole life story – falls into this window. The information here forms a wide spectrum, from fairly innocuous and nonthreatening (a favorite color or the last movie we saw), to increasingly personal and intimate (religious beliefs or health problems).

When we disclose this information, we open the "hidden" window, creating a more candid relationship and leaving less that is concealed. When we divulge secrets about ourselves we build trust in the relationship. We decide what to share, with whom and when. It is not necessary to reveal everything about ourselves to anyone who comes along. When the purpose of sharing is to build trust, select the relevant stories and experiences and share them with the intent of inviting the other person closer.

The "blind" quadrant represents things that *others know about you, but that you are unaware of.* For example, our office mate mentions we speak loudly on the telephone, something we did not realize. When she offers this feedback, she opens our "blind" window. Because this information is now out in the open, our "open" window grows larger.

These "blind spots" occur on many levels of complexity and intimacy. A neighbor may observe that we are good with children in a way we never realized; our colleagues may notice our habit of putting ourselves down when speaking in front of a group; the boss might see potential for growth that we had not realized. There is an endless amount of information in the blind window.

The opportunity for building trust by opening the "blind" window lies in our willingness to receive feedback. We do not need to accept every piece of feedback that is offered, nor is everything offered truthful or helpful. But when someone we trust has our best interests in mind, their perspective can be enlightening. These are rich opportunities to learn in public. Both parties take a step toward building trust: one by giving the feedback respectfully and the other by hearing and learning from it.

Rebra, the supervisor mentioned in Part One, used Gracious Space to get feedback on her leadership style and performance from peers and direct reports. The information she received was eye-opening, and she was able to hear it because she created Gracious Space.

"I'm a task-oriented, private person," she said. "People saw me as cold and aloof, when really I was just busy or shy. Gracious Space helped me hear that I needed to be more personable and more accessible. With one employee in particular, we had agreed to disagree for about four years. Everything was a struggle between us. When I started to be more friendly and ask about her weekend or share something about my day, she became more open in return. Our relationship is blossoming into a friendship, which is unbelievable given our history."

By being curious about and receptive to what lay behind her "blind" window, Rebra showed she was willing to learn. By sharing personal stories and gradually opening her "hidden" window to her staff, Rebra became more human and accessible in their eyes.

"My staff became more willing to be open with me and each other," she said. "They are all more supportive of me because they know me better, and I find it's so much better to work with people with this level of trust."

In the final, "unknown" window are the mysteries – *things you don't know about yourself and no one else does, either.* What is in this window? The future certainly fits here. Consequences to actions, possibilities of collaboration and long-forgotten beliefs could be included here. In this window is everything we cannot know without exploration with and through others. We need other people to unlock the mysteries of this window. The more differences that exist between us, the more there will be to uncover in this window.

The "unknown" window is an ideal place for Gracious Space and learning in public. In this quadrant we can hunt for assumptions, breakthrough ideas, buried opinions and innovative possibilities. A trusting relationship is necessary to venture into the unknown, but the converse is also true – uncovering the unknown together can build trust.

Using the Johari Window to build trust raises several questions about vulnerability and control. Who do we open up to? What do we tell them? It is important to remember that we are in charge of what we share. We cannot, however, control the reactions others will have to the information we disclose, even if we ask them to respond in a certain way. Choose the listener carefully. Choose someone who holds our best interests at heart, who can lend insight and an opportunity to learn and grow. It is an unfortunate fact that not everyone in our organizations or neighborhoods can be trusted with information from the "hidden" quadrant.

We also control when and from whom we accept feedback. When we invite others to comment on our blind spots, we need to be clear about the type of feedback we are looking for and how we want to hear it. We can request advice or not, a friendly ear, or to hear about their similar experience. Clarify any confusion and ask for examples. Getting feedback on our blind spots, especially if it is hard to hear, may make us feel inadequate, incompetent, rejected, or misunderstood. It is important to be in a good emotional state before asking for feedback. The feedback can also be something that empowers and enlightens us, uncovering fresh possibilities and options. This is the time to accept compliments, not just wave them aside. Listen deeply and think about how to build on this strength.

With the establishment of a trusting relationship by partners who are willing to learn in public, we have a ripe environment for inquiry.

gracious space journal

Building Trust

1. What is my relationship with trust? Am I a naturally trusting person, or do people need to "prove" themselves to me first?

2. How trustworthy am I? What about my character and competence earns the trust of others?

3. With whom would I like to build more trust? Why is trust with this person difficult?

4. How do I respond to receiving feedback from others?

5. How can I disclose information and give feedback to others in a way that builds trust?

6. How open is my "open" window with my workgroup?

7. What can I do to build more trust? Which windows from the Johari Window diagram will be most helpful to open?

inquiry and deep listening

"Answers are just echoes, they say. But a question travels before it comes back, and that counts."

— *William Stafford*

By now it should be clear that Gracious Space is not a model for fixing other people. It is not a strategy to narrowly define an issue. Nor is it a framework for identifying another person's vulnerabilities and using them to advance our own agendas. Gracious Space is a model for understanding other people. It is a strategy for being together while we delve into an issue to create shared understanding. It is a framework for discovering people's gifts and talents and using them to advance a shared agenda for the common good. It is both a technique and a way of being.

Unfortunately, Gracious Space is rare in our busy lives. Too often our conversations take on a hurried, scattered, or defensive quality. We spend more time advocating for what we have to say than being curious about new ideas. We need a new way to talk and be with one another. Gracious Space provides a bridge, and skills such as inquiry and deep listening help us cross that bridge.

The Center for Ethical Leadership uses inquiry and deep listening in all of its programs. Over time, we have come to rely on three techniques of inquiry and listening that will be described here: Dialogue, Skillful Discussion, and Appreciative Inquiry.

The theory behind Dialogue is foundational for the other two. For this reason, we explore Dialogue in more depth in this publication. Additional information about Skillful Discussion, Appreciative Inquiry, and other practices of inquiry can be found in the Appendix reference section.

Slow Down! Dialogue Ahead

Dialogue is an approach to leadership that highlights inquiry, reflection and listening. Of all the techniques for listening as a leadership skill, dialogue is perhaps the most counter-cultural. In addition to recommending that we slow down and listen more deeply to others, it also asks us to question our own beliefs and assumptions, in public, a lot like Gracious Space.

The root of the word "dialogue" gives some insight into why this approach is uniquely stimulating and challenging. "Dialogue" comes from two Greek roots, *dia,* meaning "through" and *logos,* meaning "word." In Dialogue, we *seek meaning* through our words with others.

The goal of Dialogue is to open up new ground – such as the "unknown" quadrant in the Johari Window – through inquiry. As we practice Dialogue, we start to pay attention to our own thoughts, to the spaces between comments, and to how ideas and people are connected. When groups inquire in this way, they generate a new level of meaning about themselves and issues they are exploring.

But inquiry can be tricky, because questions can be misleading. A question such as, "Don't you think we should do it this way?" is not a true inquiry at all. It is a leading question, one that asserts a specific agenda. A question such as, "Why do you think we should do it this way?" opens the dialogue to more possibilities and understanding. It allows one to be curious. It has the potential for creating Gracious Space. But even "why" questions, if asked simply to interrogate, satisfy one's own curiosity or defend one's point of view, will limit the learning of others. A question such as, "How can we best use our resources to do this job?" can lift one's own and other's creativity to new heights.

In today's busy world, we probably have more discussions and debates than dialogues. The word, "discussion," stems from the Latin *discutere*, which means to "smash to pieces." It has a similar root as the words percussion and concussion, meaning to knock against or hit. If our conversations feel more like a boxing match than a learning opportunity, it is probably a discussion in the true meaning of the word.

In a boxing match, the goal is to win, not to learn. Debate, discussion and advocacy certainly have their place in society, for example in political campaigns and courtrooms. But relying on this type of communication exclusively is a tremendous disservice to ourselves and others, especially when dealing with complex issues. Dialogue gives an alternative to win-lose approaches. It opens the conversation and enables us to listen deeply, even to ourselves.

According to a study reported in Please Understand Me, which describes personal tendencies and how people relate to one another, nearly 75 percent of Americans are "extroverted." This means they derive energy from being with others. When communicating they like to bounce ideas off others and talk through an issue before settling on an opinion.

This segment of the population often needs to ask questions to clarify their emergent or "half-baked" thoughts. Airtime with others, in a space conducive to reflection and learning, helps bake the rest of the idea into something meaningful and useful. The remainder of the population – the "introverts" – are people who gain clarity by reflecting with themselves. They are the ones to ask, "Can I get back to you on that?"

Dialogue provides a space for reflection for all types of people. It helps extroverts cook their thoughts all the way through with others and helps introverts clarify their assumptions and opinions before responding. In Dialogue we "suspend" judgments, figuratively hanging our judging thoughts as if we pulled them from deep water on a fishing pole. From this suspended vantage point, we can examine them more closely through the lens of curiosity. When we understand our judgments and opinions, we can decide whether to keep them or throw them back in and fish around for something else. This process is learning in public.

In Gracious Space the role of listening delves deeper than in a typical conversation. Usually we listen to gain crucial information and be on our way. Or we listen to discover how we can influence a situation, or change it. Sometimes we do not so much listen as wait to get our word in when the other person finishes.

In Dialogue, listening helps us to understand something in a completely new way. We become so engaged in listening that we often forget what our point was. Some call this generative listening, meaning listening between the lines of what is being said and building a picture in our minds; fitting puzzle pieces together to form a greater whole. One colleague who teaches at a local university used Dialogue in his classroom. He observed that as his students talked and explored with one another, the entire group's understanding bumped up a level.

Dialogue reveals the power of ideas

Dialogue and deep listening help us understand ideas in a new way and see more clearly the beauty or limitations these ideas have.

Ideas have immense power to shape our lives and we need to use them thoughtfully and wisely.

A friend traveled to East Germany in 1989 shortly after the Berlin Wall came down. As he walked through the rubble and celebrated freedom with the German people, he noticed a neon sign hanging from a crumbled building. On it was a picture of Karl Marx, the philosopher who popularized communism. Underneath Marx's image were the words: "Sorry, chaps. It was just an idea."

The sign recognized that communism was just an idea whose time was over in East Germany. During the years that the idea of communism was acted upon, it had powerful impacts on people's lives. Families, towns and nations were separated, and thousands of people died as the idea was enforced. Of course, communism the idea didn't do this by itself; the power and structures which people created on behalf of the idea led to these actions and consequences.

Nearly every system that holds our organizations and communities together is based on generally accepted ideas that are put into action. Institutions, private property, the stock market, savings accounts, social security and banks, juries, trials and jails, war, even the desire for a green lawn in the yard, are all just ideas, crafted by humans and given value and power through our actions. Practicing inquiry and deep listening helps us examine the ideas we create and the values we attach to them. We can pay attention to the power we bestow on ideas. Through Dialogue we can be more intentional and give power to the ideas that promote, not destroy, healthy work environments and communities.

Skillful Discussion

Like Dialogue, Skillful Discussion provides a tool for working with instability, inquiry and creativity. Previously we shared the root meaning of the word "discussion," which was described as a potentially fragmenting and unproductive experience. The term, "*skillful discussion*," however, promotes a different experience, one that moves beyond debate and advocacy to a collaborative process. Skillful Discussion is similar to Dialogue, in that the group is attempting to build shared meaning. The key difference involves intention. Rick Ross writes in the Fifth Discipline Fieldbook:

"In Skillful Discussion, the team intends to come to some sort of closure – either to make a decision, reach agreement, or identify priorities. Along the way the team may explore new issues and build some deeper meaning among the members. But their intent involves convergent thinking.

In Dialogue, the intention is exploration, discovery, and insight. Along that path, the group may in fact sometimes come to a meeting of the minds and reach some agreement - but that isn't their primary purpose in coming together."

This difference makes Skillful Discussion highly practical for work teams, citizen groups and other people trying to gather diverse opinion *and* chart a course of action. Below is a continuum of the different types of conversation available to us.

On one end is Dialogue, an experience where the group strives for meaning, breakthrough levels of intelligence and creativity, and as William Isaacs writes in the Fifth Discipline Fieldbook, an "aesthetic beauty of shared speech."

On the other end of the spectrum is debate, raw advocacy and

Raw Debate	**Polite Discussion**	**Skillful Discussion**	**Dialogue**

More conventional

More attuned to the sources of group thought and bringing them to the surface

the "boxing-match" type of conversations that are intended for winning and proving right over wrong. Near advocacy is "polite discussion" or "civil discourse." This type of conversation may appear to be about learning and sharing, but really it is about guarding secrets. How many times have we been in a meeting where people nod their heads in agreement, but as soon as the meeting is over they gather in the hallway and criticize? They do not share their true feelings within the meeting. The public conversations are civil and polite, but are actually fueling misinformation, resentment, and factions.

Skillful Discussion falls on the continuum close to Dialogue because it enables sharing and learning, but with the added intention of coming to a plan, conclusion or decision. When combined with Gracious Space, Skillful Discussion is an excellent approach to hold conflict and foster creativity within the workplace. Five basic behaviors are recommended for Skillful Discussion:

1. **Pay attention to your intentions.** What do you want from this conversation? Are you willing to be influenced? Be clear on what you want and do not mislead others.

2. **Balance advocacy with inquiry.** As with Dialogue, there is a need to inquire deeper into opinions and comments to surface hidden assumptions and clarify what's being said. Many teams take pride in their ability to challenge ideas and find the flaws in a proposal. This approach must be balanced with robust reflection and assumption-hunting, which will benefit the group's understanding of the issue.

3. **Build shared meaning.** Our words are symbols for our thoughts. Often we use words with multiple meanings, or which have cultural or personal nuances. Be aware of the hidden meanings behind the words and experiences being shared. What do you mean by certain terms? Is something that's "understood by all" really understood? Help others clarify what they mean by a certain expression.

4. **Use self-awareness as a reference.** It's easy to get swept up in the moment and become reactive in our conversation style. In moments when you are feeling confused, angry or frustrated, try to pause and ask yourself, What am I thinking? What am I feeling? What do I want at this moment? You may uncover insights that help the group as a whole, and you will be better prepared to present these in a respectful, authentic, non-reactive manner.

5. **Explore impasses.** Too many times a meeting or conversation ends without a clear consensus, agreement or direction. Before the group breaks up, try to determine what you agree on, and what the important facts are. Then try to pinpoint the sources of disagreement. In this way you can learn more about the situation, clarify assumptions and help the group get unstuck and move forward.

Appreciative Inquiry

Appreciative Inquiry is a process of asking questions in a way that elicits the good that already exists within an individual, group or organization. It assumes that some things, such as policies, systems, informal methods or behaviors within the system, are working well. This assumption raises curiosity about what those things are, which leads to dialogue about why they work and the conditions that support them, and finally to agreements of how to amplify them for the benefit of the organization and its members.

"Appreciative Inquiry assumes that the life-giving reality of any complex human system lies in the passion and responsibility people express in everyday decisions and activities they carry out," write David Cooperrider and S. Srivastava, who coined the term Appreciative Inquiry. "Appreciative Inquiry anchors transformational change in discovering, reporting and learning from personal stories generated within the system: stories people tell about communities or organizations working at their best."

In most organizations and communities these stories are told privately, in gossip, at coffee breaks or over lunch, or in informal sessions with family and friends. Appreciative Inquiry recognizes the public value of those stories for community building and learning. When the stories are broadcast, a community can learn what it is doing well and how to build on that.

Many traditional approaches to planned change focus on defining problems, setting targets, planning strategies, and overcoming obstacles. While such approaches have their value, they can have unfortunate side effects. People spend time focused on what is wrong rather than what is right, leading to reduced morale and resignation to a problem-filled environment. This is often called the "ain't it awful" syndrome.

Since data collection in a problem-focused approach focuses on failure, this can lead to an unconscious air of disempowerment and inferiority. People may look at the cumulative list of mistakes and errors and start to avoid risk-taking. Addressing problems can also create a culture of problem-centered improvement. In other words, the only time people pay attention to learning is when they have failed. This type of culture makes it almost impossible to engage in continuous improvement or form a learning organization.

In Appreciative Inquiry, the approach to change is to find existing solutions that work, to leverage or amplify these solutions, and focus on life-giving forces that encourage people to learn and take risks. Inquiring appreciatively doesn't take a great deal of preparation or knowledge, it simply requires an attitude of compassionate curiosity and an interest in uncovering what is good about a situation or process. The enthusiasm for what works is contagious. Spirit rises and action feels easy.

An inquisitive approach to leadership enables us to hear stories about what works in the course of our normal activities. The role of leaders is to frame questions that elicit the depth of people's interests and passions, and to respond with genuine interest and enthusiasm. We collect essential details of the stories and examples, and connect to the storyteller through empathy and active listening. We learn what excites the other person and are in a position to support that. We can encourage the teller to expand, to connect beyond the specifics to how the whole community could benefit from what works. Sample questions for Appreciative Inquiry can include:

- What's good about this idea/system/process?

- Why is that important to you?

- What's working you'd like to tell me about?

- Why do you enjoy this work?

Dialogue, Skillful Discussion and Appreciative Inquiry are three tools to foster inquiry and deep listening. They each help create Gracious Space, and can be used in conjunction with other tools to advance understanding and action on a particular issue.

gracious space journal
Inquiry and Deep Listening

1. *Is my dominant communication style to pose questions or advocate for my beliefs?*

2. *When I ask questions, what is my tone, and what kind of questions do I usually ask?*

3. *How do I respond when someone questions me, my opinions, my knowledge, or my experiences?*

4. *How interested am I, really, in learning more about other people's ideas? What behaviors do I display that communicate this interest?*

5. *How might I undermine my desire to learn? In other words, what behaviors do I engage in that can shut down inquiry and deep listening?*

6. *How willing am I to "suspend" my ideas and judgments and have them examined? By myself? By others?*

challenges of gracious space

"Nothing would astonish me, after all these years, except to be understood."

— Ellen Glasgow

From the many stories we hear from individuals, communities and organizations, Gracious Space is clearly a needed and welcome approach for leadership. Why, then, doesn't it happen more readily? Why does Gracious Space have to be created? There are many barriers to Gracious Space, some of which we have already covered, such as personal vulnerability, mistrust and fear, lack of interest in differing view points, lack of time, or a dominant culture that supports a different style of communication and problem solving. The personal awareness required for Gracious Space can be demanding.

It is also true that some tools of Gracious Space are not necessary for every situation. Inviting diverse viewpoints and learning in public are systemic approaches that create more complexity before reaching a decision. Sometimes this is unnecessary, and too many opinions can get in the way of effective leadership. The solution may be clear and we may simply need to communicate the goals and facilitate the work. But at the Center for Ethical Leadership, we believe that the skills of Gracious Space are underutilized in today's busy workplaces and communities. So when the situation calls for a more systemic approach, try to invite the "stranger" and learn in public.

Once in Gracious Space, there are some unique considerations. One is the extra time it can take compared to more traditional methods. It takes time to figure out who are the "strangers" and encourage them to participate. Developing trust and the skills to use Gracious Space effectively can result in a more lengthy process. Another caveat with Gracious Space is that it can be hard work. Listening – truly listening and not just preparing your rebuttal – can be consuming. Gracious Space encourages us to listen, not just reload. Being open to diverse perspectives is a learned skill that requires patience and practice. It is far more difficult to work with others who are different from us.

Recently a colleague had an opening in her department and was torn between two qualified, but very different applicants. One had less experience, but a friendly and service-oriented style that would have fit well within the established group. The other candidate had more experience and better skills, but a more abrupt working style. My colleague was tempted to hire the more friendly, coachable employee because the similarities would have created a more enjoyable workplace. But she hired the other individual. She believed her team and their results for the organization would be stronger with the second person's different point of view. These are difficult choices and the leader ultimately has to decide the approach that works best for the team and for the organization.

It is also possible that some could perceive Gracious Space as a wishy-washy or weak approach to leadership and decision making. As leaders, we are expected to have a "firm" leadership style and know the answers. But that is not always possible. Our job in these situations is to help others see how Gracious Space is a valid, result-oriented and useful approach. We need to demonstrate the value of diversity and how a more systemic approach can illuminate a complex issue. As one CEO we work with put it, *"The 'soft' stuff is the hard stuff."*

As we embrace Gracious Space, we need to be aware of these potential hazards and take steps to deal with them. We will likely fall back into old patterns now and then. We need to take ourselves less seriously and have a sense of humor as we gain skills in Gracious Space. Patience and a willingness to reflect on failures and successes will go a long way in becoming more effective at creating Gracious Space.

part two review

- Trust, inquiry and deep listening help Gracious Space to thrive.

- Trust is measured by what is possible when it is present.

- Disclosing information and receiving feedback help to build trust.

- Practicing inquiry and deep listening can help us to look at the ideas we create and the values we attach to them. Doing so helps us be more intentional about giving power to ideas that promote, not destroy, the common good.

- Approaches such as Dialogue, Skillful Discussion and Appreciative Inquiry are different from our habitual ways of relating with one another because they strive to uncover new meaning in an appreciative setting.

- Dialogue is primarily used when the group is seeking to expand its understanding and the aesthetics of ideas. Skillful Discussion is used primarily when the group seeks to expand its knowledge and take shared action. Appreciative Inquiry is an effective way to discover what works, and build on that.

- There are unique challenges to creating Gracious Space, including time to gather and discuss diverse ideas, and the hard work of deep listening.

- The tools of Gracious Space are not necessary in all situations. They can be systemic in nature and biased toward big-picture thinking. When this is not needed, use a different approach.

- Gracious Space has the power to change our lives and the organizations and communities we work in.

part three:

gracious space in action

"As life is action and passion, it is required of man that he should share the passion and action of his time, at peril of being judged not to have lived."

— *Oliver Wendell Holmes, Jr.*

The Center has had the opportunity to introduce the concept and skills of Gracious Space to many individuals, groups and organizations. They have taken the idea, added their own twists and have generated creative and powerful applications of Gracious Space in real situations. This section describes some applications of Gracious Space in the spirit of celebrating "best practices," but also to offer practical hope for readers wanting to apply Gracious Space to their own issues.

personal applications

Using Gracious Space at a personal level can include giving yourself Gracious Space and creating an inner practice, and it can include your relations with others.

In Part I we met Rose who was struggling to get along with her aunt at the family reunion. This scenario was based on a true story, and Rose went back to the reunion determined to find a way to connect with the aunt in a more positive way. When she returned, Rose told us that she created Gracious Space and told her aunt how she felt about the personal questions. The aunt was surprised, wanting only to feel connected to her niece, and agreed to a new type of conversation. Their relationship was transformed. Rose was very excited as she described their new connection, and was getting up her courage to introduce Gracious Space at work.

Janine Larsen, principal consultant with Manage to Serve, a Washington-based organization that works with nonprofit agencies, incorporated Gracious Space into her practice. "I think people feel Gracious Space emotionally, at a soul level," she said. "I have become more conscious of creating a presence that communicates my values as much as my words and symbols. It holds open the door to the rest of my message."

"I have used Gracious Space while visiting relatives, standing next to my friend's two rottweilers, and by giving myself Gracious Space," said Allen Taylor of Seattle Public Utilities. "When you give Gracious Space to yourself, your feet no longer always follow your head every place your head wants to go. You enter a more spiritual place where your heart is more dominant in the decisions you make. That's when you have learned to give yourself Gracious Space."

Judy Hansen, Manager of Employee Learning at Swedish Medical Center in Seattle, describes her application of Gracious Space.

> *"The biggest application I have had of Gracious Space was about learning in public. In some of my previous work I felt great pressure to have all the answers and be the expert. I recently came into a large organization and it was important for me to understand others' approaches. Gracious Space helped me understand my role in a different way and be willing to learn, with others, in public.*
>
> *"I am much more comfortable admitting in a group that I don't know the answer or even the questions. I listen to their ideas and we come up with a decision together. It has been enormously freeing personally, and the results are better for the organization. I am so pleased with the response of my team to the idea of learning together – we are creating Gracious Space for each other."*

When I first tried to bring Gracious Space into my relationships, I was not very graceful. I grew increasingly frustrated at dinner conversations where everyone talked over each other, giving opinions on topics we really knew nothing about. As my friends threw conjecture like confetti at a wedding, I blurted, "Can you please just let people finish!" Their stares implied that this rapid back-and-forth was a normal dinner conversation, and there must be something wrong with me. I didn't know how to convey my underlying desire for a more engaging conversation. I was simply trying to get them to slow down so we could all be more thoughtful. Gradually, I learned to ask questions in a way that helped everyone, including myself, think more fully about what we were saying.

People have written to the Center describing how they used Gracious Space with neighbors, to relate to their children, and at work to give themselves breathing room when they were uncertain about taking the next step. The uses for Gracious Space in our personal lives are limitless.

organizational applications

Using Gracious Space in organizations is helpful on a number of levels. In the introduction we described Boeing's desire to learn cutting-edge leadership skills and navigate in an uncertain business climate. They have recently formed an informal group to explore internal issues such as ethics and personnel development, using Gracious Space as a container for their conversation.

We also learned about Seattle Public Utilities' leadership program, which helps employees claim their leadership role in the utility. SPU recently launched an Alumni program for the more than 200 graduates of the program. Alumni come together in Gracious Space to resolve some of the agency's most complex business issues. "We need a diverse set of perspectives to make better business decisions," said Chuck Clarke, director of Seattle Public Utilities. "It's important to provide a level of Gracious Space so we can share the risks, stresses, and mistakes, and raise issues without having negative consequences."

Jeannette Bliss, Human Resources Director for Hopelink, a human service agency in Bellevue, Washington with 200 employees, describes how the directors used Gracious Space during a difficult budget season. Donations were down and the budget was undergoing cuts. Nevertheless, directors wanted to honor their two core values: serve the clients and reward a hard-working staff that hadn't seen a raise in some time. The directors decided to use Gracious Space during the four-month budget process.

"We kept our core values in front of us and we were able to have conversations we couldn't have had before," said Jeannette. "There was a lot of honesty and trust, and none of the 'why didn't you do it this way' type of suspicious questioning. The open process helped us put all the possibilities on the table, being respectful of each other's budgets and department needs, and look at the whole. We didn't have any 'meetings after the meeting' and consequently we came back with some really good solutions. Gracious Space helped us make some really difficult decisions." Their work resulted in one of the more creative and thoughtful budget cuts in the history of the organization, and the public responded with understanding and support.

Ahna Machan, former director of the Education Foundation of the Associated General Contractors of Washington (AGC), related the following story on how skillful discussion helped the AGC explore difficult issues and make better decisions.

AGC is the state's oldest, largest and most powerful commercial construction trade association. In 1998, AGC members identified leadership education as a top goal in their strategic plan. Three years later, the AGC Board of Trustees, committee chairs, and department managers participated in the AGC of Washington Leadership Institute. The Leadership Institute explored communication, and explored the benefits and differences between debate, polite discussion, skillful discussion and dialogue. Most AGC contractors used a communication style that enabled them to quickly identify a problem and find a solution. Problem-solving is extremely valuable in the construction industry culture and is responsible for many business successes. However, the members were involved in several situations where direct, rapid problem solving was not effective. They were open to expanding their competencies into other styles of communication.

The AGC officers used skillful discussion at a Board of Trustees meeting to discuss the complex and volatile issue of ergonomics. In the past, a committee would meet in advance, discuss the issue, and bring forth an analysis and recommendations. Trustees would *politely* discuss the issue, and approve the recommendations without a deep or collective understanding. After the meeting, dissatisfaction would ferment until it rose to the surface and the entire issue had to be revisited.

At the board meeting, skillful discussion guidelines of inquiry, clarifying, and reflecting were emphasized. Members were encouraged to listen to various aspects of the issue rather than advocating for one position. They moved past joking about the new skills to awkwardly trying to use them. This created a space for open dialogue where Trustees voiced differing positions, probed for more information and asked questions to understand each other's intent. It was a spirited discussion, and the meeting lasted twice as long as anticipated, but everyone felt heard and satisfied with the decision. Months later AGC members still proudly talked about the way they made the decision and the Gracious Space that allowed for open discussion and collective understanding. They continue to use skillful discussion at their Board of Trustees' meetings, tackling fewer issues but exploring them with more depth and understanding.

community applications

Our neighborhoods and communities are ripe environments for applications of Gracious Space. Due to the diversity inherent in community, there is often a need to involve many different people in a very public decision making process. Gracious Space provides a vehicle for inclusive community involvement.

Sherry Tiggett and Tanya Nelson describe an on-going community effort sponsored by the W.K. Kellogg Foundation. The new Kellogg Leadership for Community Change (KLCC) program was launched in 2003, and coordinators recognized that participating communities would need to create an environment in which the participants could respect and trust one another and the group process. They adopted Gracious Space as the way to create this social environment to foster respect, effective leadership, and successful teamwork.

One KLCC group at Flathead Indian Reservation in Montana wanted to identify ways to reduce the dropout rate among high school students on the reservation. The group encompasses 28 individuals representing a wide range of ages, social, economic, racial, and cultural backgrounds, and includes teachers, college and high school students, parents, education administrators, tribal leaders and local business owners, among others.

Harry Goldman, community coach for KLCC's Montana fellows, said the fellows are using Gracious Space as a way to hold each other in mutual respect.

> *"There are many factors at work within this community that (can) lead to division. Groups are identified that take sides regarding social, political and cultural issues. It becomes very easy to stereotype members of an identified group which leads to misconceptions, false assumptions and distrust among individuals in the community. Fellows come from both the Indian and non-Indian groups and under normal circumstances some of them would not choose to work together.*

*"By engaging each other in a Gracious Space and allowing
the stereotyping to be discarded through listening to each other's
personal stories a common ground was established and mutual respect was able to develop. The notion of 'winning' through debate
is unacceptable."*

It took three or four meetings before the fellows began to fully
understand and embrace the Gracious Space concept. Once they did,
members were willing to speak from the heart and the relationships
within the group took on a new and deeper emotional dimension, Goldman says.

The Gracious Space concept corresponds well with KLCC's goal of
breaking down barriers that can impede cooperative problem solving.
At Flathead, the Gracious Space concept and set of norms have already
begun to transform the way fellows interact beyond the group. The
fellows share a passion for teaching and learning, and are trying to find
ways to shift the public will around education and develop dropout
prevention activities that are appropriate to their local situation. The
fellows plan to share the most effective strategies with all the schools
on the reservation, in Montana and those affiliated with the National
Indian School Board Association.

In a second example, the City of Seattle created a city-wide program for neighborhood planning around the theme "grow with grace."
Karma Ruder, former director of the city's Neighborhood Planning
Department, describes the impact the principles of Gracious Space can
have on a larger community.

Neighborhood volunteers led their own planning processes, a
method intended to emphasize individuality and ownership by citizens. At the outset, one of the biggest fears was that the program
would fall into the trap of some previous citizen planning efforts,
which had merely churned out the recommendations of the last five
people standing.

Phase One focused on inquiry to develop shared understanding
and consensus around the major work that neighborhoods wanted
to advance. Two incentives encouraged volunteers to reach out and
ask questions: 1) they could not get Phase Two funds unless the plan
represented all the different interests surfaced in Phase One, and 2) the
plans would not be approved unless they had broad neighborhood support. Some of the questions volunteers asked during Phase One were:

- Who isn't at the table that should be? What do they think is important?

- What kind of outreach will entice people to come and share their thoughts?

- How do we make newcomers feel welcome?

Neighborhoods that stepped up to the challenge of inquiry and listening created a strong and diversified foundation for their work. They created relationships that withstood the confrontational and challenging work of making choices among alternative options. Some methods of listening included:

- Panels of people with different viewpoints, followed by group conversation;

- Storyboards describing situations in the neighborhood and seeking feedback on approaches to address the issues;

- "Written conversations" recorded on large paper during community meetings;

- Giving children cameras and having them make a visual map of their neighborhoods;

- Surveying people at food bank lines; and

- Going to events of community members who hadn't attended a planning meeting to seek out their opinion.

In one neighborhood, leaders argued that the volunteer group was already representative of the neighborhood and they did not need to bring in others. If others did not choose to participate, they said, then those who were there should be able to do the plan.

However, the lure of Phase Two funding and the desire to shape the future of their neighborhood (rather than leaving it to city staff) motivated them to recruit new members to better represent the diversity of the neighborhood. They then they had to struggle through a challenging process, as the question about what was best for the neighborhood resulted in conflicting answers.

At the end of Phase One, the leader presented the work to the City Council. He said he was exhausted and that it had been the hardest work of his life. He said it was worth it, however, because the neighborhood had been transformed and was more connected and collaborative than he had ever thought possible.

In another neighborhood with a highly divisive history, the neighborhood leaders embraced the new approach. The neighborhood became more unified than ever before. They leveraged millions of dollars for neighborhood investment because they were clear about their values and priorities.

part three review

- Gracious Space can be applied at a day-to-day level of awareness, and at a more systemic level with groups and communities.

- The personal applications of Gracious Space are infinite, and include relationships with family, friends, colleagues, neighbors, strangers, and cultivating a spirit of Gracious Space within and for ourselves.

- Gracious Space used within organizations has dramatic and constructive results. Groups respond positively to the freer flow of information, are more apt to try to learn from each other and more likely to take risks and turn "mistakes" into learning opportunities.

- Gracious Space has a helpful and unique role in difficult decision making and situations where conflict is likely. It can diffuse the tension and invite a more honest level of exchange.

- In communities, where diversity is prevalent and democratic decision making is desired, Gracious Space can create norms and guidelines to help the group work together better.

conclusion

This publication has attempted to describe the core elements of Gracious Space, how to create it, and how to put it to use. We have also shown, through real examples, the impact Gracious Space can have on individuals, organizations and communities.

We have seen that the range of actions and emotions associated with Gracious Space are broad. We can adopt some personal behaviors and strive to live Gracious Space at a day-to-day level by being kind, by nurturing our inner spirit, and by listening with curiosity. We can also use Gracious Space in a more systemic method to delve deeply into complex issues with diverse thinkers in our organizations.

Creating Gracious Space is a very strong act of leadership. Leading in a way that invites union, rather than incites discord, requires strength and vision. This is the work of our time. The instruments of peace and understanding are in our possession, but they only play for us when we pick them up and use them.

appendix

gracious space self-assessment

Gracious Space: Gracious Space is a spirit and setting where we seek the stranger, and where we embrace learning in public.

Below is a list of values and behaviors that are helpful when creating Gracious Space.

<u>Circle</u> those you feel competent with. <u>Star</u> those with which you are less comfortable. Choose one or two you want to improve and intentionally bring these into your work and relationships with others.

Establishing norms

Interjecting humor/fun

Affirming others

Being open to feedback

Accepting different perspectives and ideas

Innovating new approaches

Being present

Being aware of my impact on others

Assuming others' best intentions

Being intentional

Being reliable

Trusting others

Being trustworthy

Willing to change my mind

Willing to slow down

Reflecting on assumptions

Actively seek others opinions

Being curious

Asking open ended questions

Discerning patterns emerging from a group discussion

Learning and sharing rather than just advocating

Listening deeply and generatively

Willing to be influenced

Being comfortable receiving lots of questions

Being comfortable not knowing

Able to detach from outcomes

Being collaborative

Capable of stopping, reassessing and redirecting

Fascinated/curious about differences

Being open to differing and conflicting views

Welcoming others not in my comfort zone

Being compassionate

Empowering others

Being authentic

Feeling comfortable with community wisdom

Building community

Bridging boundaries

Extending respect to everyone

Sharing power

Seeing everyone as gifted and capable

Holding off on judgment

Steering conflict toward positive, creative results

guide for getting started

The following tips will help you make Gracious Space a reality in your life, family, organization or community.

Tip #1.   **Make a personal commitment** to the spirit of Gracious Space: intention, compassion, and curiosity.

Tip #2.   **Involve others in a dialogue on the meaning of Gracious Space.** Create group norms or agreements on how the group will work together based on their definitions of Gracious Space. Be sure to include open and honest conversation.

Tip #3.   **Complete the Gracious Space Self-Assessment.** There are many behaviors and skills associated with Gracious Space, and the Self-Assessment will help you discover your strengths and areas for improvement. Write the areas you want to improve on a sticky-note and attach it to the refrigerator, computer or dashboard to remind yourself daily.

Tip #4   Invite others to complete the Gracious Space Self-Assessment and share their strengths and learning goals. Team members can support each other in achieving their learning goals, and you will **create the beginning of a learning community**.

Tip #5.   Identify elements in your "hidden" window and **disclose some information** with the intent of building trust. Invite feedback into your "blind" windows.

Tip #6.   Commit to **"inviting the stranger" to your next important meeting**. Determine whose voice has not been heard, or someone who has a very different perspective on your project, and bring this person into the dialogue. Be sure to explain your motivation, use welcoming language and set aside enough time for a meaningful exchange.

Tip #7.   **Model Gracious Space** at home, in the workplace, and in the community, even in traffic, or when your grocery line is moving more slowly than all the others.

Tip #8.   **Acknowledge and reflect on actions that demonstrate Gracious Space.** For example, at staff meetings ask members to acknowledge acts of Gracious Space they have observed of each other.

summary of gracious space protocols

- Pay Attention to Spirit

- Clarify Your Intent for Setting and Interactions

- Invite the Stranger

- Learn in Public

- Build Trust

- Inquire

- Listen Deeply

dialogue building blocks
from *The Fifth Discipline Fieldbook* by Peter Senge

Dialogue has four main building blocks, which if practiced, can change how a person views their own thoughts and the perspectives of others.

1) Balance Inquiry and Advocacy. Ask "why," be curious, and spend as much time asking questions of yourself and others as you do relaying your ideas and opinions.

2) Surface and Identify Assumptions. Go "assumption hunting." Dig deeper, go fishing, and ask what lies behind an idea or concern.

3) Suspend Judgment. When you discover assumptions, hang them high for all to see. What can you learn from them? Upon further inspection, do you want to keep them or let them go in favor of something new?

4) Generative Listening. Listen between the lines. What is emerging in the spaces between? Try to put the puzzle pieces together to form a greater whole. How is the group's understanding improved?

some behaviors that support the dialogue approach include:

- Be willing to be influenced by others

- Explore assumptions

- Speak to the center of the group

- Listen to my "chatter" or how I respond internally

- Let go of being right

- Speak to the center (avoid cross-talk)

- Be curious

- Invite differences

- Seek the next level of understanding

- Slow down

- Speak when moved to speak

groupthink

Groupthink typically occurs when groups are highly cohesive and when they are under considerable pressure to make a quality decision.

Some negative outcomes of groupthink include:

- Examining few alternatives

- Not being critical of each other's ideas

- Not examining early alternatives

- Not seeking expert opinion

- Being highly selective in gathering information

- Not having contingency plans

eight main symptoms of groupthink

1. **Illusion of Invulnerability**: Members ignore obvious danger, take extreme risk, and are overly optimistic.

2. **Collective Rationalization**: Members discredit and explain away warnings contrary to group thinking.

3. **Illusion of Morality**: Members believe their decisions are morally correct, ignoring the ethical consequences of their decisions.

4. **Excessive Stereotyping:** The group constructs negative stereotypes of rivals outside the group.

5. **Pressure for Conformity**: Members pressure any in the group who express arguments against the group's stereotypes, illusions, or commitments, viewing such opposition as disloyalty.

6. **Self-Censorship**: Members withhold dissenting views and counter-arguments.

7. **Illusion of Unanimity**: Members perceive falsely that everyone agrees with the group's decision; silence is seen as consent.

8. **Mindguards**: Some members appoint themselves to the role of protecting the group from adverse information that might threaten group complacency.

ten ways to avoid groupthink

1. The group should be made aware of the causes and consequences of groupthink.

2. The leader should be neutral when assigning a decision-making task to a group, initially withholding all preferences and expectations. This practice will be especially effective if the leader consistently encourages an atmosphere of open inquiry.

3. The leader should give high priority to airing objections and doubts, and be accepting of criticism.

4. Groups should always consider unpopular alternatives, assigning the role of devil's advocate to several strong members of the group.

5. Sometimes it is useful to divide the group into two separate deliberative bodies to evaluate feasibilities.

6. Spend time surveying warning signals from rival groups and organizations.

7. After reaching a preliminary consensus on a decision, all residual doubts should be expressed and the matter reconsidered.

8. Outside experts should be included in vital decision making.

9. Tentative decisions should be discussed with trusted colleagues not in the decision-making group.

10. The organization should routinely follow the administrative practice of establishing several independent decision-making groups to work on the same critical issue or policy.

further reading on aspects of gracious space

Nurturing Spirit
Leading from Within, article by Parker Palmer
Let Your Life Speak by Parker Palmer
A Different Drum by M. Scott Peck
A World Waiting to Be Born by M. Scott Peck

Building Trust
Jack Gibb on Trust: www.geocities.com/toritrust
Personal Village by Marvin Thomas
Living in Truth by Vaclav Havel

Conflict Resolution and Negotiation
Getting to Yes: Negotiating Agreement Without Giving In
        by Roger Fisher and William Ury
Expand the Pie: How to Create More Value in Any Organization by
        Grande Lum, Irma Tyler-Wood, Anthony Wanis-St. John

Inquiry
"Mindwalk: A Film for Passionate Thinkers"
        (based on Fritjof Capra's The Turning Point)
Public Conversations Project:
        http://www.publicconversations.org
The Thin Book of Appreciative Inquiry by Sue Annis Hammond

Deep Listening
Horton Hears a Who by Dr. Seuss
A Dialogue for Freedom by Vicki Robin
*The Lost Art of Listening: How Learning to Listen Can Improve
        Relationships* by Michael Nichols

Dialogue
On Dialogue by David Bohm
Changing Consciousness by David Bohm and Mark Edwards
DIA*logos Incorporated
        http://www.dialogos-inc.com/index.html
Dialogue by Glenna Gerard and Linda Ellinor

about the Center for Ethical Leadership

The Center for Ethical Leadership cultivates leadership and builds the capacity for change, by helping organizations and communities tap local wisdom in service of the common good. We invite people to reach across boundaries, build trust, and lead from their core values to advance change. By convening diverse perspectives—especially those historically excluded—we are creating healthier, more just, and inclusive communities.

We are the pioneering ethical leadership organization in the Pacific Northwest, building collective leadership capacity for those advancing social change around the country. Founded in 1991 by Dr. Bill Grace, the Center has engaged thousands of people across the United States and from more than 35 countries.

The Center frequently brings diverse people together to learn, explore, and work for the common good. We create the conditions for personal and collective transformation through innovative models, programs and approaches such as Gracious Space. Our approach to leadership has proven effective in a variety of settings, including tribal nations, rural communities, urban neighborhoods, and communities of color.

Our collective leadership and community change work across the country led to the founding of the Community Learning Exchange in 2008. This network brings together resilient communities, vibrant organizations, and active change agents to share their local wisdom and collective leadership approaches with each other so they can be more effective in addressing critical social issues. You can join this network of change agents at www.communitylearningexchange.org.

The Center is a nonprofit corporation in the State of Washington. Visit us at www.ethicalleadership.org.

References

Bohm, David. <u>On Dialogue</u>, transcription from Ojai California,1990.

Chittister, Joan. <u>Scarred by Struggle Transformed By Hope</u>, Grand Rapids Michigan Wm. B. Eerdmans Publishing, p.107

Cooperrider and Srivastva. "Appreciative Inquiry in Organizational Life," in <u>Research in Organizational Change and Development</u>, William Pasmore and Richard Woodman Editors, Vol. 1, p. 129-169, Jai Press, Greenwich, CT, 1987.

Covey, Stephen. <u>The 7 Habits of Highly Effective People</u>, Fireside, New York, 1989.

Cuomo, Kerry Kennedy. <u>Speak Truth to Power: Human Rights Defenders who are Changing our World</u>, Crown Publishers, New York, 2000.

Fenhagen, James C., <u>Mutual Ministry</u>, Harper & Row, New York, 1977.

Gibb, Dr. Jack. <u>Trust: A New Vision of Human Relationships for Business, Education, Family, and Personal Living</u>, Newcastle Publishing Co; Revised edition, 1991.

Grace, Bill. <u>Ethical Leadership: In Pursuit of the Common Good</u>, Seattle, WA 2001.

Greenleaf, Robert K. <u>Servant Leadership: A Journey into the Nature of Legitimate Power and Greatness</u>, Paulist Press, New York, 1977.

Heifitz, Ron. <u>Leadership Without Easy Answers</u>, Belknap Press, 1994.

Hemingway, Ernest. <u>A Farewell to Arms</u>, Simon and Schuster, New York, 1929.

Isaacs, William. <u>In The Fifth Discipline Fieldbook</u> by Peter Senge, Currency Doubleday, New York, 1994.

Janis, I. L. & Mann, L. <u>Decision making: A Psychological Analysis of Conflict, Choice, and Commitment</u>. Free Press, New York, 1977.

Keirsey, David and Bates, Marilyn. <u>Please Understand Me: Character and Temperament Types</u>, Gnosology Books, 1984.

King Jr, Martin Luther. Correspondence, "Letter from a Birmingham Jail," April 16, 1963.

Kofman, Fred, Ph.D. Conscious Business, audiotape published by Sounds True, Boulder, CO, 2002.

Laszlo, Ervin. The Choice: Evolution or Extinction? A Thinking Person's Guide to Global Issues, G.P. Putnam's Sons, New York, 1994.

Luft, Joseph. Of Human Interaction, National Press Books, 1969.

MacGregor Burns. Leadership, Harper Collins, New York, 1978.

Macy, Joanna. World as Lover, World as Self, Parallax Press, Berkeley, CA, 1991.

Mink, Dr. Oscar G., Developing and Managing Open Organizations: A Model and Methods for Maximizing Organizational Potential. (With J. Shultz and B. Mink), University Associates, La Jolla, CA, 1979.

Palmer, Parker. Spirituality and Education. Paper presented at Seattle Pacific University, Seattle, WA, 1989.

Perich-Anderson, Jagoda. Creative Conflict: Generating Innovative Ideas, Seattle, WA, 2000.

Ross, Rick. In The Fifth Discipline Fieldbook by Peter Senge, Currency Doubleday, New York, 1994.

Roosevelt, Eleanor. You Learn by Living: Eleven Keys for a More Fulfilling Life, Harper, New York, 1960.

Senge, Peter. The Fifth Discipline Fieldbook, Currency Doubleday, New York, 1994.

Senge, Peter and Lannon-Kim, Collen C. Systems Thinking Newsletter, 1991.

West, Cornel. Speech at the First AME Church, Seattle, September 10, 2004.

Other books by the Center for Ethical Leadership:

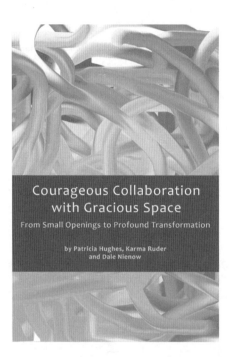

<u>Courageous Collaboration with Gracious Space</u>, by Pat Hughes, Karma Ruder, and Dale Nienow. This book describes the Gracious Space Change Framework, a powerful and proven approach to hold our differences, dialogues and dreams so we can invent a more positive future together.

<u>The Collective Leadership Storybook: Weaving Strong Communities</u>, edited by Karma Ruder. This book describes the patterns of working together that encourage collective leadership. Read about communities where people made these patterns a way of life to advance the common good.

To order these, or any of our publications, please visit our website.

www.ethicalleadership.org